# Guppies, Bubbles, and Vibrating Objects

## A CREATIVE APPROACH TO THE TEACHING
## OF SCIENCE TO VERY YOUNG CHILDREN

# Guppies, Bubbles, and

## A CREATIVE APPROACH TO THE TEACHING

## John McGavack, Jr.

# Vibrating Objects

## OF SCIENCE TO VERY YOUNG CHILDREN

## Donald P. LaSalle

**THE JOHN DAY COMPANY / New York**

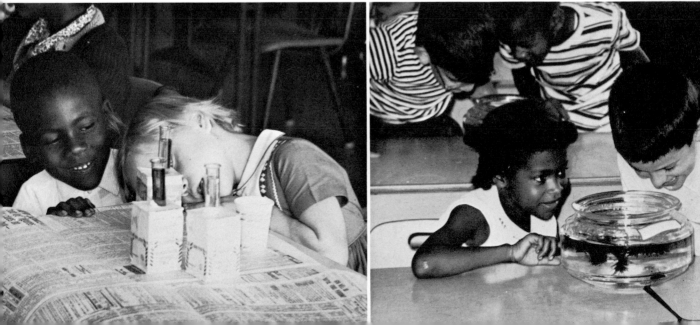

ACKNOWLEDGMENTS

The authors are greatly indebted to the teachers, students and
administration of the Avon and New Haven Public Schools and
in particular to Sheldon Glick and John Dommers for their excellent photographic work.

Library of Congress Catalogue Card Number: 69-10805

Printed in the United States of America

# Preface

Young children are akin to scientists in that both possess insatiable curiosity about the world in which they live. Our intention is to have young children, freely exercising this built-in curiosity, explore new and exciting paths opened by the teacher, all the while using simple and easily available materials. The authors maintain that a creative approach to the teaching of science means making it possible for children to behave in the classroom in ways very similar to the way true scientists themselves operate.

Using science units that have been successfully tested with primary children, we present here what we consider is a guide to the development of workable science programs adaptable to varying local needs. The first section, captioned *"How to Begin,"* constitutes a point of view embodied throughout. A second portion is devoted to *"Why Do It This Way,"* in which a justification for this particular approach is explored. The nucleus of this book, the third section deals with the nuts and bolts of really designing child-oriented science experiences. It is appropriately labeled *"How to Do It."* Last, an entire section is devoted to resources for the teacher and student and covers the broad spectrum from reading materials to science equipment and audio-visual aids, and is called *"Where to Find Out."*

This book can serve two major functions. One is as an instrument used in preparing prospective teachers for teaching science at the primary level and the other is as a ready guide for classroom teachers already engaged in the daily task of guiding primary children in their classroom experiences. Every effort has been made in this book to aid teachers in developing materials, experiments, and investigations which will permit students an opportunity to uncover as well as discover the excitement and wonder of science. The immediate goal is to get science happening in as many classrooms as possible throughout the nation. The units herein are planned with this thought in mind and have been designed to permit children many chances to make mistakes and to use their senses in creating, experimenting, analyzing, measuring, recording, and observing while having fun in the process.

Many activities have no real ending but are left to the imagination of both teacher and student. It is our intention to "stir children up—not tie them up."

John McGavack, Jr.
Donald P. La Salle

# Contents

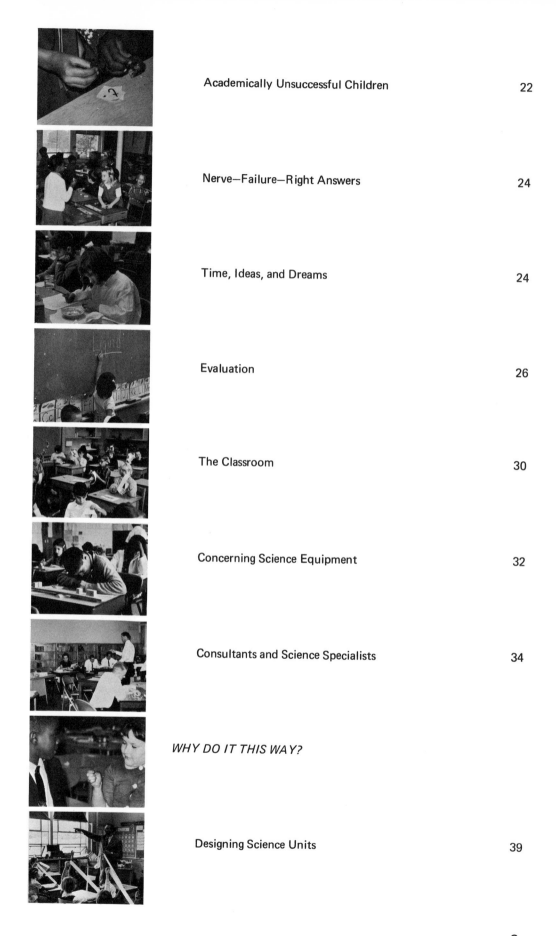

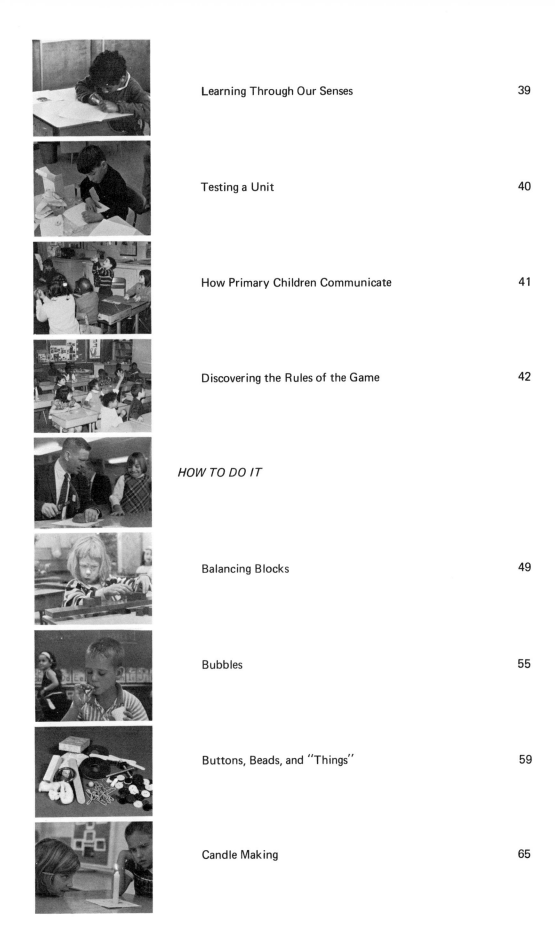

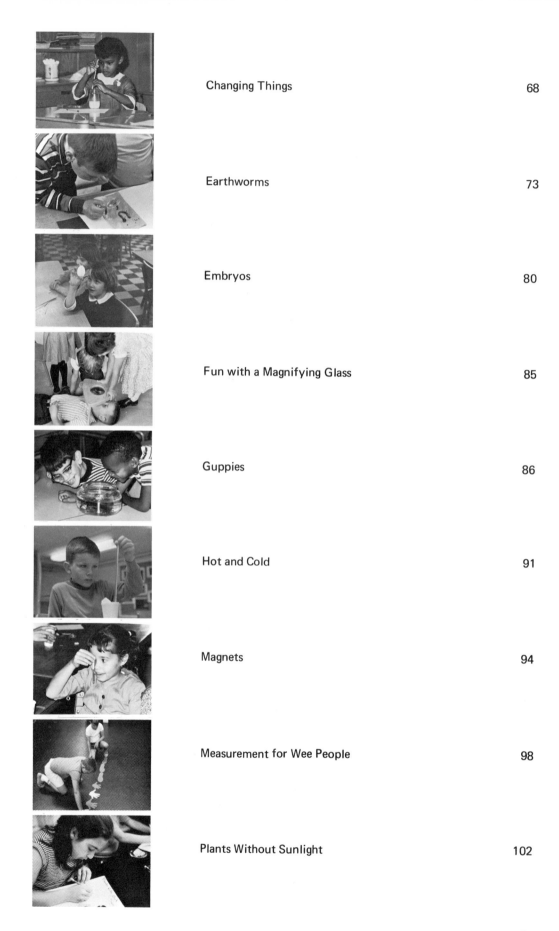

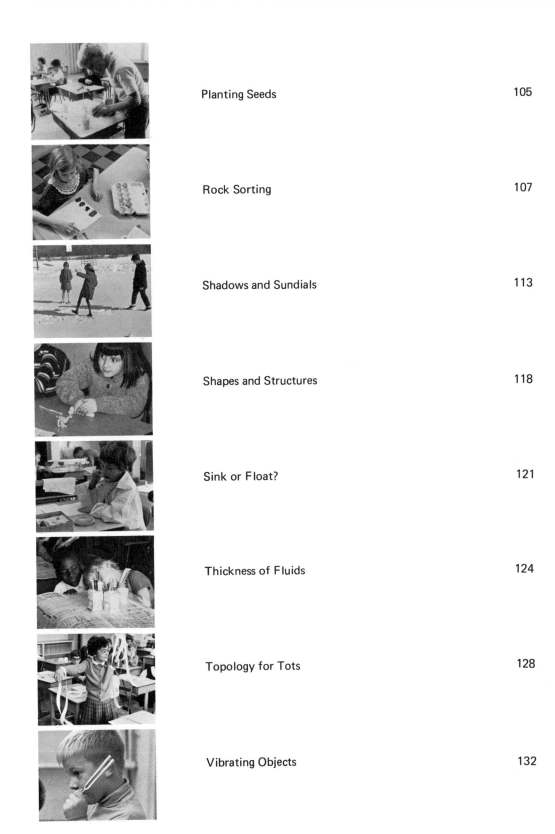

*WHERE TO FIND OUT*

# How to Begin

# How to Begin

We often hear that the shadow cast by a school system is the length and breadth of the man at the top—we hasten to add that the success of any school system depends on the teachers within it. In the singleness of its purpose and organization it can be claimed that the educational system is unique.

A thoughtful consideration of a particular school system will show that there isn't any other place quite like it. We say this because its professional staff are all trying to do things which have not been done before, and their output is mostly paper, expression, and ideas. They produce no "hardware" for industry. They sell nothing in the public marketplace. The paper referred to may be the idle drawings of a third grader, the finger paintings of a first grader, a lengthy report on Newton, a set of mathematical problems, a spelling list, or an extensive research paper. These actions are all quite different from those, say, of the telephone companies, with which we all deal every day, because their point of view is one of providing a service, whereas ours is one of stimulating fresh thinking patterns, motivating greater self expression, and developing understanding and tolerance which ultimately will contribute to the fullest development of a human being.

### An Overview

Hy Ruchlis, a well-known curriculum expert in the field of science education, has described the problems of the elementary school teacher as follows:

The problems of the elementary school teacher are substantially different from those of the high school teacher. Whereas the high school teacher is expected to be a specialist in one or two subject areas, the teacher of elementary grades is expected to be reasonably competent in geography, history, arithmetic, art, music, and science, and is also expected to know something about the psychology of children and their parents, baby care, and housekeeping in the classroom. Quite frequently, the elementary school teacher is a bookkeeper charged with handling funds. And all this must go on in a relatively small room in which 30 to 35 wiggling young children are to be kept simultaneously interested in teacher-directed activities for a period of 5 hours a day. When you stop to think of it, it's a wonder that the teacher actually accomplishes so much.

That is not to say that the life of a high school teacher is a bed of roses. It isn't. He has his own problems—but of a different kind. However, when we view the actual teaching situation in the elementary schools we no longer wonder about why science is not taught, but rather begin to think about how we can help the teacher do the kind of job that needs to be done in science.[1]

Experienced elementary school teachers are generally aware that organized science programs from kindergarten through the intermediate grades are relatively new in the curriculum. Until perhaps the advent of the first orbiting Russian satellite in 1957, when America suddenly became aware of encroaching technology and its potential impact on school curricula, science was the stepchild of elementary school instruction. As a result of Congressional legislation beginning shortly thereafter, new, promising, and exciting science curricula were developed which attempted in some way to lessen the lag between learning and the learner.

Most were the fruits of considerable labor involving experienced personnel from all parts of the education spectrum. The early new curricula had for the most part two things in common: they were unquestionably departures from traditional approaches to the teaching of science, but they

[1] Hy Ruchlis, *Developing Concrete Experiences in Elementary School Science and Mathematics* (New York, Harcourt, Brace & World, A School Department Newsletter, Spring 1966).

tended to concentrate on the high school level.

It soon became clear, however, that a revolution in educational thinking geared toward improving science programs in today's schools would have to begin at the **beginning.** We could no longer afford to regard science in the elementary school as a conglomeration of haphazard experiences offered on a strictly hit or miss basis.

Suddenly the elementary school teacher was confronted by a virtual plethora of teaching guides, segmented curricula, and varied suggestions concerning the direction such change in science teaching should take. Generally, the major stress, with which the authors heartily agree, was upon involving youngsters in science and not upon content and the accumulation of factual information. Fortunately, the pendulum had begun to swing and curriculum developers concentrated on the previously neglected elementary levels.

On the other hand, little has been done to educate or enlighten the already overburdened elementary classroom teacher, who is often tossed new curricula and complex programs and directed to implement these without the benefit of a short workshop or consultant service. To fill this need is the purpose of this book.

### Attitudes

A good program of science instruction for young children must do more than acquaint students with facts and content. It should resist turning students into **walking encyclopedias of supposedly important scientific information.** Instead, the greatest concern should be with helping children **to learn how to learn** rather than with having them just follow the rules of the game as prescribed by the teacher.

In the final analysis, while the factual and content areas are important, the **skills and techniques,** or, more simply, the **investigative know-how,** are of paramount importance. Content can serve as the vehicle by which the skills may be learned and not just the end to justify the means.

An ancient Chinese proverb suggests an attitude for science instruction in the elementary schools:

*I hear and . . . I forget*

16

*I see and . . . I remember*
*I do and . . . I understand*

## Scientific Method—the Formula?

One area of concern that has need for further explanation is the frequent reference made by many teachers to the **scientific method**. The following statement, taken from the unit "Mealworms" (developed by the Elementary Science Study), does much to clarify an often confused term.

It is not true that progress in science is invariably achieved by employing the scientific method. Probably few scientists make real progress by adhering to the scientific method or, for that matter, to any set method. As a useful tool the scientific method can be best employed only when one has the clear advantage of hindsight: it is of little help when one needs foresight.

Though the scientific method is by and large unused during creative moments, it is later employed for reporting the research, and it is the context in which the reader learns what has happened. For when a paper is presented, so neatly does each step lead to the next that one may be left with the impression of a scientist as a man who thinks on a plane of complexity no layman can ever share. What rarely, if ever, reaches the reader are: first, the elements of luck, frustration and hunch playing that are involved in research; and second (and perhaps more important), the fact that almost without exception important contributions to science are not incredibly complex ideas but beguilingly simple ones arrived at by beguilingly simple paths of reasoning. The complexity lies not in the reasoning process, which is simple at any level, but in the accumulated experience with which one approaches a problem.

In making these disparaging remarks about the scientific method, we certainly do not wish to imply that it has no value. The rigor it imposes has been uniquely responsible for the evolution of science into the powerful discipline that it has in fact become. The scientific method is essential to science, but in teaching only that to students one is teaching them about the history of science and not about the way that scientists think. When a scientist finds occasion to concern himself with the scientific method, he is being the critic, not the creator of an idea—whether that idea is his own or someone else's.

Children should not be taught that science can only be carried forward by selected people with extremely clever wits. They should begin to realize that the sorts of experiments they themselves devise, if carefully done, are often just as good as those performed by other people called scientists. It should not be thought, however, that there is nothing worth learning about how to approach problems. On the contrary, one of the things students should gain from an education in science besides a background of information is an appreciation of the fact that certain approaches are likely to be more fruitful than others.

For many years the teaching method in science has been the following formula: observe, hypothesize, test. There is nothing wrong with this formula except that it is not enough. Consider a collection of blocks—all the same color but different shapes (cubes, rectangles, diamonds, spheres, etc.), sizes (large and small cubes, rectangles, diamonds, etc.), and made of various materials according to shape and size. The primary child will observe this set of blocks, but he may focus on some minor or insignificant property of the set; for example: he may observe that one or two of the blocks are dirty from handling. The intermediate-grade child will hypothesize but may choose the wrong variable for testing and end up not knowing what to do next; for example: he may hypothesize that all the blocks have different weights and choose size as the determining variable to test this hypothesis, only to be confused when some big blocks seem lighter than smaller blocks. He may choose the correct variable for testing, **obtaining positive results**, but not know what to do with his results; for example: he may hypothesize that all the blocks have different weights, choose one shape to test this hypothesis and arrange them according to weight (determining that some smaller blocks are heavier than some larger blocks), but not conclude that the blocks are made of different materials. The middle-grade youngster can formulate propositions, based on his testing, but may not know how to combine his propositions systematically so as to test all possible combinations of the variables involved; for example: he may propose that the blocks are made of different materials, according to shape and size, but find it difficult to set up the combinations (material, shape, and size) for meaningful testing procedures. An approach to science teaching can be synthesized out of the observe-hypothesize-test formula. This synthesis requires clever yet patient teacher guidance—not structured unimaginative teacher direction. There is room in this **formula** for **minor or insignificant observations, testing of wrong variables, and unsystematic combinations of propositions.** The teacher can synthesize from the **formula** meaningful student-centered science learning, provided this formula does not become an end in itself, but rather a vehicle to stimulate exciting individual patterns of observing, relating, and thinking.

The following quotation from a national curriculum project in elementary science provides additional support for this approach.

Science is more than a body of facts, a collection of principles, and a set of machines for measurement; it is a structured and directed way of asking and answering questions. It is no mean pedagogical feat to teach a child the facts of science and technology; it is a pedagogical triumph to teach him these facts in their relation to the procedures of scientific inquiry. And the intellectual gain is far greater than the child's ability to conduct a chemical experiment or to discover some of the characteristics of static electricity. The processes of scientific inquiry, learned not as a set of rigid rules but as ways of finding answers, can be applied without limit. The well-taught child will approach human behavior and social structure and the claims of authority with the same spirit of alert skepticism that he adopts toward scientific theories. It is here that the future citizen who will not become a scientist will learn that science is not memory or magic but rather a disciplined form of human curiosity. From the start the child is an active participant in these scientific tasks. He does, indeed, **observe, classify, measure, predict.** He has the chance to work as a scientist by carrying out the kinds of tasks which scientists perform.[2]

**Science Curriculum Reforms**

The curriculum reformer is eager to supply the teacher with new materials and to get into the classroom and provide teacher training in their proper use. The result of this effort is hopefully an end to rote learning and boredom and the birth of excitement, discovery, and student experimentation. More attention must be accorded the teacher and in particular an understanding of the pressures imposed on the teacher by parents and school administration to get the children to **know** the material important for that grade. These pres-

---

[2] American Association for the Advancement of Science, *Science—A Process Approach Description of the Program,* Part A., Washington, D.C., 1967.

sures do not make it more difficult for the teacher; on the contrary, rote learning and adherence to a strict curriculum schedule, while not exciting for either the children or teacher, do establish a pattern that is easily followed year after year. **Breaking** into this pattern is the difficult task of the curriculum reformer. The average teacher usually will pose the following question when confronted with a new approach: "Oh no, **do I have to teach the children something new in addition to the regular material we are supposed to cover?**" This question is usually followed by another: "**What is the new material they are supposed to know?**" The average teacher is not ready to **waste** time on new approaches because there is not enough time to cover the required material. Teachers with this attitude, whatever the real cause, will not try new materials enthusiastically. When they do try new materials their attention will always be focused on getting the material completed (making sure the the new material is **learned** so they can return to the work that must be covered). People constantly ask, "**Why don't they teach those kids what they are supposed to know?**" or "**What's all this 'discovery' nonsense?**" Certainly, untestable learning—at least untestable by usual testing patterns—such as use of materials for free exploration and discovery "**won't help these kids learn to spell, read, multiply, etc.**" according to such skeptics.

The curriculum reformer must do more than supply new materials and train teachers in their use. He must also find ways to cope with the dilemma of balancing certain expected standards, imposed on schools by internal as well as external forces. The new material, which by its very structure stresses process rather than facts, attacks the time-honored mode of teaching and learning. The curriculum reformer must effectively balance ideal goals against the realism of internal and/or external forces in his attempts to make resourceful and powerful curriculum materials more than just fragments of information parceled out in rote learning exercises.

Dr. Eugene Howard, Director of Innovation Dissemination for IDEA (Institute for the Development of Educational Activities), stressed the important difference between

superficial change and basic change when he stated:

Innovation, if it is to amount to something, must be more than mere organizational manipulation, must involve a change in what teachers do when they teach, what students do when they learn, and what they both do when they interact with one another. Critical thinking, inquiry, and self-directiveness must be made a part of the curriculum.[3]

The school should be inquiry-oriented with the teacher functioning as a stimulator, diagnostician, prescriber, environment planner, and materials organizer. The student in this school would function as an inquirer, object manipulator, idea organizer, explorer of curious phenomena, generalizer, discusser, and communicator of ideas and conclusions.

[3] Excerpt from address by Dr. Eugene Howard given at the National Seminars on Innovation, Kamehameha Schools, Honolulu, Hawaii, July, 1967.

The increased desire of school districts to plan their own programs, coupled with moderate gains in teacher ability and desire to teach science, has reduced complete dependency on the use of conventional science textbook series. However effective the text material, the sole use of a text can force a structured program that limits the scope of topics in the science curriculum. Increasing numbers of schools and school districts are organizing their science programs without science textbooks and are investing their budgets in equipment and library materials which accommodate the versatility and individualization of their curricula. (Non-basal, Multi-level Reading materials.) Totally new activities must be developed where the nature of the activity and the equipment utilized will permit full physical involvement of all students. Increased imagination of authors and publishers to provide other than conventional textbook material will be required to maintain and increase effectiveness in elementary science education.[4]

## Textbooks

Science is a **doing activity**; it is not static. Current textbooks for science attempt to present science as a doing activity, but for the most part do not fully achieve this goal. The real problem with a textbook is that it does a magnificent job of **departmentalizing** learning. Dr. Elizabeth Wood, an eminent crystallographer, has this to say about science textbooks: "They should be written like murder mysteries—instead they are written in quite the reverse manner. In most textbooks you are told who committed the murder on page one and then for two hundred pages thereafter you are told how it was done." It is no wonder that the majority of these texts fall short of their objectives. The following statement is a brief summary of current thinking on the role of textbooks in the classroom.

## Inquiry, Observation, and Laboratory Experience

There is much being said about the **inquiry** or **discovery** method of science teaching. It is refreshing to note that this method is receiving such concentrated attention, although the implications resulting from this attention are rather disturbing. One implication is that science has suddenly changed from whatever it used to be to a discovery or inquiry kind of activity, and because of this change, we in the schools had better present science in the new form it has now assumed. The basic methods have not changed, for individual discovery and inquiry have always been fundamental to science. This approach is new to the teaching of science in our schools, not to the scientists in their laboratories! It is fortunate that we are

[4]Paul F. Ploutz, "Trends in Elementary School Science," *Science & Children's Magazine,* National Science Teachers Association, Washington, D.C., February, 1965.

now attempting to teach in our schools the way science has always been, not the way it seems to to have just suddenly become.

Science education cannot assume, as it has up until now, that elementary school children have developed the beginnings of adult understanding and require only concentrated exposure to fundamental laws as embodied in current science curricula. Most elementary children, as well as many adults, do not have the ability to organize the understanding that they have arrived at from the raw materials of experience. This ability is not acquired through the memorization of many related or unrelated facts about nature. Nor is it acquired through science curricula that merely list basic concepts the teacher is expected to convey at specific grade levels and that children are supposed to assimilate by some magical means.

In all child-oriented classroom activities the ingredients must be **equipment for each youngster, the statement of a problem to which individual responses and solutions are desired, and a patient and competent teacher.** Within this structure new questions will arise, leading to further explorations and experiences from which other questions will be formed. **The laboratory should not be considered merely as the place where questions are answered, but rather as the place where, most of the time, questions are shaped.**

Contrary to common belief, it is more difficult to teach a class in which equipment and materials are in abundance than one where materials are in short supply. In the latter case, class control is relatively easy. All children see the same demonstrations. All react at the same time. All are simultaneously reacting to the same teacher questions. In a situation where materials are plentiful and children are permitted time to manipulate equipment independently, class control is much more difficult. Each child now sees the result of his own explorations. Each child now is free to react differently because of his individual ability to use the equipment. Responses are not simultaneous or in unison; the class noise level is greater, and class control obviously presents a special challenge, but the rewards are great. It is in this kind of classroom atmosphere that the child can experience excitement of learning.

Children should be placed in situations that require them to make decisions. Some of these decisions may or may not be meaningful. But, is it important that all decisions be good or meaningful? Cannot the process of merely making a decision have a beneficial outcome? A child's ability to make decisions depends on his reaction to his present situation and his ability to organize meaning out of raw experience. This ability will improve when the child is allowed to practice making decisions based on raw experience.

Youngsters will improve their ability to think, relate, and observe if given time to practice thinking, relating, and observing.

### Reading Level

How often have you heard the statement "**Those kids can't do that—they can't read**"? It seems that in classes where the general reading level is below grade level many activities and experiences are put aside until "**we get them up to reading level.**" The attitude revealed by this statement appears to be related to the idea that the classroom day must be subdivided into special packages of time: a time for science, a time for history, a time for spelling, a time for reading, a time for arithmetic.

Subdividing the school day into fragmented pieces coupled with low reading levels usually results in little or no time to relate similar learning experiences. How about using science as a **vehicle**

to motivate youngsters to want to read, spell, multiply, and verbalize? Cannot reading, spelling, and mathematical skills be integral parts of science experiences? To improve reading, is it always necessary to start with the reading book?

The poor reader, who is frequently categorized as a slow student, can often deal with concepts and ideas. He can be motivated to be curious and enthusiastic and to develop a free, questioning attitude. Science represents an area through which the stigma of "poor reader" may be overcome, provided the school is willing to devote the time and patience to stimulate these children in other methods of individual expression.

## Academically Unsuccessful Children

The focal point of all curriculum is its ultimate effect on the development of the individual. Curriculum must be developed and implemented in a manner such that each individual can actively participate and identify his role in the successful completion of a classroom experience. It must be broad enough to span the entire student ability spectrum yet personalized enough to permit children to understand their individual roles in its successful accomplishment. Present trends in curriculum development place greater emphasis on student involvement with materials. Children exposed to this emphasis may not react as expected or with enthusiasm. Most curriculum is seemingly developed for the middle- and upper-middle-class child. The lower-class child from disadvantaged environments is frequently considered a risk—**a risk in the sense that he cannot be trusted to manipulate and/or care for equipment in an "acceptable" manner.** These are usually children who read well below

grade level, are behavioral problems, difficult to interest in conventional activities, in general a major source of trouble to the teacher.

Strict discipline has been the conventional way to remedy problems unique to these children. Certainly, freedom of physical activity and independent use of classroom materials have usually been considered unsatisfactory practices. Basically, children are quick to react in accordance to the methods employed during their early development. Teachers are quick to stereotype children. Once a youngster has established a "reputation" it is extremely difficult to change it or the effect it will have on other teachers. Therefore, a troublesome, uncooperative child (earlier labeled a "risk") remains such in the eyes of most teachers. If he is given the opportunity to manipulate equipment, and subsequently breaks it, teachers usually respond, "I told you so, he just can't be trusted." Their predictions were not unfounded and there is general self-approval of their ability to judge children.

What did they expect? Such teachers get back exactly what their teaching methods produce, a youngster incapable of dealing constructively with materials because he has never been given the opportunity to practice using the materials or equipment. Children are quick to know what behavior patterns are expected of them. They are adept at discerning the teacher's feeling of their "place" in the behavioral structure of the class and usually respond accordingly.

Considerable attention is currently focused on the disadvantaged child. What curriculum materials should be used? Disadvantaged youngsters do not need a different substance for their education. They can learn concepts, manipulate materials and equipment, formulate ideas, and express opinions. They can be enthusiastic and curious, and practice creative thinking. All of the worthwhile student-centered activities of any learning situation can be just as real and meaningful to disadvantaged youngsters as they are to any other youngsters. **The substance need not be different, but the approach must be different.** These youngsters need a great deal more encouragement, direct experience, and experience with success. Progress is slower and teacher patience must be unlimited.

Perhaps the term "disadvantaged" is not the most descriptive, and should be replaced by "academically unsuccessful." There are many classifications. No matter what the classification by different investigators, the one shared characteristic of all groups is lack of success in school activities. Recent research leads to new assumptions about these students and their role in the learning situation. The most important of all these assumptions is that everyone can learn, provided he is given the opportunity to develop confidence and self-respect.

Although the following list[5] was formulated primarily for high school students, it also depicts realistically the characteristics of the academically unsuccessful student at all levels. Teachers must accept the challenge of developing a school program that utilizes the known potential of these students and hence results in a successful educational experience for them.

What do we know about the student who has not and is not profiting from the conventional school program? What do we know of him that is relevant to helping him gain from his school experience?

One or more of the following are often characteristic of the academically unsuccessful student as he is seen in school:

1. He has difficulty dealing with symbols, particularly written verbal and mathematical symbols.
2. He has not learned basic skills necessary for dealing with written language and quantitative relationships; i.e., he has difficulties with reading, writing, and mathematics.
3. He has difficulty concentrating on school tasks.
4. He has difficulty in expressing in oral and/or written language what he does know and think.

5. He has difficulty realizing the significance of what he is asked to learn.
6. He is unwilling to carry school activities beyond campus, e.g., homework.
7. He has difficulty in taking tests.
8. He is antagonistic to school and school authority.
9. He is convinced he can't learn, but at the same time seems to refuse to acknowledge his academic problems.
10. He is a behavioral problem.
11. He has a poor attendance record.
12. He is apathetic and indifferent.

But the student who possesses one or more of the above characteristics has often demonstrated his potential in some of the following ways:

1. He is able to cope with a very difficult environment; e.g., a child who is capable of surviving in a slum environment must have considerable stamina and ability.
2. He is very inventive in the use of non-standard oral language.
3. He is able to progress and to be successful when dealing with things in which he is interested; e.g., understanding the complexities of a modern automobile engine.
4. He is able to concentrate for long periods of time when dealing with things of interest to him.
5. In some optimum academic situations, he has been successful; e.g., Higher Horizons and More Effective Schools programs of New York City.
6. He shows considerable insight into human behavior; e.g., he shows considerably more maturity and ability to function in various social situations than do many highly academic "straight-A" students.
7. He imaginatively attempts to frustrate the school system.
8. He is creative, that is, approaches and deals with various situations in unusual or unconventional, but appropriate ways.

[5] Biological Science Curriculum Study—Special Publications No. 4.

### Nerve—Failure—Right Answers

The following true story should stimulate some thoughtful consideration about the nature of our teaching methods and the school systems charged with this overwhelming responsibility.

A particular class was just starting the first lesson of a **Balancing Blocks Unit.**

In this unit, each youngster is given a board two feet long, a fulcrum, and eight small blocks. Essentially, what each student does for approximately six weeks is to manipulate the blocks in different positions, while at the same time keeping the board balanced on the fulcrum. Raw experience is accumulated, and in time the student tries to generalize from this raw experience, developing some qualitative and/or quantitative rule about the **balancing situation.** In this class the first lesson of the unit was just starting. The first lesson sheet asks each youngster: "Can you balance the board on the fulcrum?"

All the students, except one, successfully balanced the board on the fulcrum in several ways. This particular student had tried *once,* failed, and would not try again. The classroom teacher urged him to try again but he would not. During the teacher's conversations with this youngster, another boy walked over, abruptly picked up the board, quickly balanced it on the fulcrum, and disgustedly said, "**There, you dope, that's how you do it.**" This abrupt intervention apparently motivated the reluctant youngster to become actively engaged in the balancing activity, for he ultimately did very well in the unit. It was later learned that this boy was a brilliant lad. The interesting point in this story is that this youngster did not have the **nerve to fail.** In this classroom he had always been the **academic leader.** He had always gotten the **right answer.** He had seldom failed, and hence he did not have the **nerve to fail.** As it turned out, his contemporary who offered him assistance was not labeled a bright student. He was accustomed to failure, and consequently he did have the **nerve to fail.**

Do teachers have the **nerve to fail?** Do school systems have the **nerve to fail?** Are teachers and the systems they represent apprehensive of change or new situations because they do not have this **nerve to fail?** Have external and internal pressures caused school systems to lose their **nerve to fail?** Have they abdicated this right to failure because of community pressure, or because of the lack of imaginative and daring leadership at all levels? The truly great intellectuals and leaders of all ages have been able to cope with failure. Certainly the scientist in his laboratory, the mathematician seeking new numerical relationships, or the historian piecing together fragments of events in years past all must have had **nerve to fail.** Thomas Edison is reputed to have tried at least one thousand different substances in his attempt to develop a filament for the first incandescent light bulb. An associate remarked that it was a pity that they wasted so much time on materials that had failed, to which Edison replied, "**Nonsense, we didn't fail—instead we now know one thousand substances that won't work.**" In the example of the youngster who refused to try to balance the board, the sterile conditioning process of his previous school years had shaped a personality whose major concern was for **right answers** or **teacher approval;** too little time had been devoted to **experimenting in learning.**

### Time, Ideas, and Dreams

A former high school physics student majoring in engineering physics at college revealed some interesting thoughts in one of his letters. It contained the following paragraph:

This has been a fairly busy year. Being my fifth, the pace has slackened a little for I have "only" five courses this term. This allows me to take a little time out to do some thinking rather than the usual grind-out-the-problems-no-time-to-think work which has become nearly intolerable over the past three years and made me dislike school. This year I have discovered again that I can think after a several year dormancy, so I am much happier. I have also built into my schedule some folk dancing—my first real extracurricular activity since I had to give up track after freshman year. What with all these improvements, I find that I am tending toward becoming human, and it's great fun.

The problem of finding time to reflect and evaluate raw experience is not unique to one level of the educational establishment—all levels share this responsibility. In our elementary schools is where we begin, but in our higher institutions the pressure of consuming more facts and concepts must not prevent us from continuing. In considering the amount of time necessary to accomplish effective teaching of science at the primary level, an approach toward integration of subject matter could be the key. Excluding specific time periods that are necessary for laboratory investigations, the discussion of science content and concepts should not be limited to any set time. In the primary grades students often spend most of the school day with one teacher. Opportunities to answer questions that arose earlier may be handled more effectively later in the school day.

Practically no aspect of our daily existence takes place without involving some area of science. Consequently, confining science experiences just to special periods of the school day is unrealistic. There is a tendency today to overdepartmentalize knowledge. When this practice is applied to school curricula the result may be a stagnant and stereotyped program. Just as one cannot separate in one's thinking the beauty of a leaf on the tree from this same quality when observed on the ground, so one should not consider the biology of the life processes independently of the chemistry of these same processes.

Lastly, the interest and desire of the students

themselves as they work on their investigations should decide how much time is actually needed.

As alert educators we must deal with ideas. A good idea, a complete new thought, must come from an individual. It may be added to by a second person, but one cannot have half an idea. How does an individual get an idea—one that no one else has had?

Can you remember as a youngster seeing some boy reprimanded for being a no-good daydreamer? Today in education it is our business to encourage some dreaming, some aimless play; in fact, at times, instead of scheduling every minute of each day with some activity, we suggest leaving a block of time that could be labeled "aimless play." But, who is to say when aimless play is not fruitful?

There are times when we must let our imaginations run wild; from this will come new discoveries by properly trained and motivated people. Einstein is reported to have said that knowledge is not very important; it is imagination that counts! What he probably meant is that if all knowledge could be written in books and placed in a library, perhaps nothing would come of it. Only if it is placed in the minds of individuals who will use it imaginatively will it bring new understanding, new discoveries, on which the progress of the human race is based.

The following definition of imagination, attributed to the English translator John de Trevisa, in the year 1398, is a nice definition because it illustrates man's eternal struggle to get away from the **here and now**, to see beyond the horizon—to dream.

Imagination is that faculty whereby the soul beholdeth the likeness of things that be absent.

### Evaluation

Evaluation is an important part of the teaching procedure. Teachers must give more than casual concern to current testing techniques. In any curriculum, evaluation cannot be ignored. It does little good to design imaginative curriculum materials and to educate teachers in their productive use if classroom evaluation procedures virtually undermine the objectives and aims of the new curriculum programs. There is no point in talking about the acquisition of certain skills, and developing exciting approaches directed at learning the **process of science**, if our testing methods make no effort to deal with these points but instead insist on the **regurgitation** of detailed information upon command.

Teachers must concern themselves with the difficult task of writing evaluative questions which measure the aims and objectives of a curriculum. It makes little difference who writes the textbooks or educates the teachers, for in the final analysis those who control the evaluation procedures largely control the curriculum content. This is why it has become increasingly important for classroom teachers to place emphasis on an area

that has long been neglected. Considerable time and energy must be devoted to learning how to construct test questions properly, questions that adequately measure the aims and objectives of a curriculum. We must recognize that the material to be tested goes far beyond the routine memorization of facts. A new perspective is needed to permit the teacher to span the unimaginative chasm of most testing procedures and develop the willingness to experiment with the testing of **process and attitudes**.

A few general questions about evaluation require consideration.

1. Can progress be evaluated without the use of a formalized written measuring instrument?
2. Can content and process be measured simultaneously? Can they be measured independently?
3. Are content and concept evaluations similar?
4. To what degree does form (organization) affect the ultimate results of evaluation?
5. How does past experience affect our approach to the evaluation process?
6. Is evaluation motivated largely by parental and/or school administration pressures?
7. Is evaluation a necessary final activity for all learning processes?

Every day we classify and evaluate **conditions** of our environment. We offer sweeping evaluations of our neighbors and business or social contacts. Frequently we hear statements such as "Jim is a good man"; "Oh, yes, he is a very responsible lad"; "He is a very successful businessman"; "She sews beautifully"; "A very competent person." The bases for remarks of this sort do not always stem from a large collection of personal **raw experience**. Nevertheless, they are the result of some experience and certainly support our willingness to accept **raw experience** as the foundation for evaluation. The classroom and its collection of children form a **unique set** from which we daily collect and classify raw experience, which we knowingly or unknowingly evaluate without the use of a formalized written evaluative procedure!

It is possible to consider evaluation for content the simplest of all evaluative procedures. Evaluation for content does not always imply understanding of content. When understanding and content are linked together in one evaluative device, the evaluation procedure immediately becomes much more complex to devise. The strictly content-oriented evaluative device encountered in many classrooms today requires only the recall of certain memorized facts. The following is an example of this kind of "test":

1. Light travels in a straight line. True or False?
2. The closer you are to a light, the brighter it appears. True or False?
3. What happens to light when it passes through a prism?
4. White light is made of what basic colors?
5. Material which does not permit white light to pass through it is called _____.
6. You cannot see objects clearly through some materials (translucent). Name some.
7. A magnifier makes objects appear larger because it bends the light. True or False?

This test could be rewritten in the following manner, so that understanding and content are more evenly balanced.

1. Below is a picture of a light source and a pencil. Draw the position of the shadow cast by the pencil.

2. In which direction would you move the pencil to produce the darkest shadow?
3. Where in relation to the prism below must you be to see red light? Mark an "R" where you would stand. Mark a "B" for blue light.

4. You are standing close to a very bright light, as shown in the diagram:

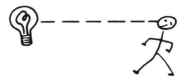

(a) If someone turned off the light when your eyes were closed, could you tell that the light was off?

(b) If you had sunglasses on and you had your eyes closed when someone turned off the light, could you tell that the light was now off? Would it be easier to determine than in (a)?

(c) If you were standing far away from the light, would that change your answer to (a) or (b)?

5. A magnifying glass bends light, making objects appear larger. A thick lens will bend light more than a thin lens will. Which lens will make objects appear larger—A or B?

$0_A$    $0_B$

Evaluation of any kind should lead to the formulation of searching questions which ultimately will provide considerable student-centered participation and stimulation. The evaluative procedure then becomes more of a class activity than a competitive exercise in which all that matters is checking the **right answer**.

Content and concepts can be measured simultaneously. It is preferable to design situations where they are considered in this fashion. It is probable that in most classrooms content is measured independent of concept understanding.

Process need not be linked to content. The process employed by a primary youngster in classifying objects according to size, shape, or color is the result of independent action motivated by past experience or present impulse. The scheme or pattern developed is an indication of an **individualized process** which the teacher wants to observe, encourage, and develop. **Process is not so much taught as it is learned.** Process implies confrontation—confrontation with situations that permit the practice and development of a youngster's ability to make raw experience meaningful.

Ideally, the most efficient as well as the most difficult evaluative device to develop is one in which there is a delicate balance between content, concepts, and process. Each can be considered independently. It is the blend of all three which most school systems proclaim as their ultimate goal in the preparation of an **educated individual**. Putting into classroom practice this blending of content, concepts, and process is a difficult task. Teachers with the **courage** to practice this blending, realizing that **mistakes** are inevitable, will accept the responsibility of shaping the patterns of learning experiences for all youngsters in the educational establishment.

The routine mechanics of administering and organizing the form of an evaluative procedure require more than casual concern. Evaluations should not be so crowded with directions and instructions as to cloud the objectives of the evaluative device. Certainly you have often heard the remark "**It's good to practice learning how to take a test**"; or, "**One must get accustomed to the testing situation.**" Remarks of this sort seem to imply that it is the **testing situation** which is of greatest concern, not the content, concepts, and processes the test is designed to evaluate. Organizing an evaluative device in a simple straightforward manner and creating a relaxed classroom atmosphere will place more emphasis on the content, concepts, and processes in the tests and less on the pressure of the **testing situation**. The evaluative or **testing situation** need not be a **pressure-packed** traumatic period of the school day. Usually it is the teacher's organization of the evaluative device and the manner in which it is made a part of the daily classroom organization that creates fear, anxiety, or apprehension in the minds of youngsters. How often have classroom teachers offered the following response to an unattentive class: "**You better listen because I am going to test you on this material next week**"; or, "**You better know this or you will fail the test next week.**" The evaluative device becomes the **club** that is used to motivate learning. The teacher who uses this procedure reinforces personal fears and fosters anxieties and apprehensions about the testing situation. Possibly, the frequent use of the **club** will result in

youngsters becoming immune to its threat and the associated tensions. In either approach the true value of an evaluative procedure is completely destroyed. To be sure, questions are asked and questions are answered, but certainly very few new questions are shaped from such procedures.

Individuals generally react to situations in terms of their accumulated past experience. The teacher's past experience with evaluative procedures tends to shape present approaches to evaluation. College students preparing to be teachers are frequently confronted with the dilemma of reconciling how the professor actually handles the evaluative procedure in his own classes with how he says it should be considered in the elementary or high school situation. The old cliché "**Do as I say, not as I do**" frequently appears to be true. Past experience can be modified by present experience, but once a mold has been created from previous experiences, for some teachers the present is no longer powerful enough to effect any change.

To what degree do pressures external to the classroom motivate formal evaluation? Parental pressures regarding evaluation are a reality, but the degree of parental concern varies between school districts. Rules for dealing with specific situations are impossible to devise. The teacher's evaluation of a child's progress ultimately must be a judgment decision. This judgment decision is substantiated by a collection of quantitative and qualitative information. For the beginning teacher the assignment of grades is one of the most trying experiences. There are many doubts—the adequacy of tests, the level and extent of emphasis in certain classroom work, and the number of formalized evaluative periods, and more. The beginning teacher is inclined to be introspective in struggling with the first assignment of grades. The more experienced teacher seems to have fewer problems with the **grading situation**. Indeed, this is a result of more experience in collecting evaluative data and using it to carefully meet the **grading situation**. The more experienced teacher does run the risk of being less introspective about his procedures than the beginning teacher. Concern motivated by introspection must not be overlooked. Perhaps a beneficial result of parental concern about grades may be the rebirth of an introspective attitude.

Earlier it was stated that **evaluation is an important part of the teaching procedure** and that **teachers must give more than casual concern to current testing techniques.** This is true, yet should all teaching procedures be followed by an evaluation? In fact, might not one of the testing techniques be no test, no evaluation? In many respects teachers attempt to overevaluate or to insure that most classroom situations are ones that easily lend themselves to some form of student progress evaluation. **Does a particular science unit always have to end with an evaluation? In a sense, must we always tie in the loose ends—summarize the results? Why not let some of the loose ends dangle? Some activities may be good intrinsically. Are conclusions always necessary?**

Probably the most important feature of a particular science experience is the change it produces in the children who have participated. These changes, besides the straight knowledge of content, are in the category of new skills and attitudes. For example: Has curiosity been stimulated? Are more questions asked? Can predictions be made? Is attitude more critical? Can new tests be designed? How is information correlated? Any effective evaluation must seriously consider these questions.

Conclusions, evaluations, or summaries should not always be thought of as the necessary final activity for all learning experiences.

Many teachers are reluctant to let pupils draw their own learnings from an experience. Instead, they feel they should summarize at the end of a period what has happened and what they intended the children to learn. This unfortunate tendency is so common among teachers that it has been given a name, lysiphobia—the fear of leaving "loose ends." Besides forcing on the children conclusions they are not capable of assimilating, this tying-up things in a neat package cuts off the gradual growth in understanding which comes when the children try out their glimmerings of new ideas or other experiences at school

and at home. In fact, it is probably worthwhile to do the contrary, to stir up any conclusions the children have reached by reminding them of the incompleteness of their understanding—of unanswered questions or of ambiguous interpretations.[6]

Perhaps we should be more rightly concerned with stirring children up instead of tying them up—instead of insisting on regular summaries or evaluations.

Robert L. Kent, Indiana's State science supervisor, believes that one good way for a teacher or supervisor to evaluate a particular science program is to check on participation in extracurricular activities by students. "Certainly a school band, whose members practice only during a few short class periods, will not march in the big parades," he comments. "Nor will the athletic team that skimps on its hour of class time win trophies or championships. When are we going to recognize that a truly successful science program also extends beyond the class period? How many kids come back for more?"[7]

Teachers attempting to teach science in the elementary school by the process approach or the laboratory method often ask the same question: **"How can we evaluate the students' progress if some investigations are open-ended and we cannot insist on right answers?"** Perhaps we should not be so concerned with just right answers but rather with the interest, motivation, and outright zeal with which a youngster will attack a problem when he is allowed to draw conclusions based upon his own observations. The alert teacher can probably evaluate a student's progress more realistically by simply watching closely the way in which the child operates under these new conditions. It is not necessary always to have something concrete in the form of an objective evalua-

[6] Robert Karplus, *Elementary Science Study Newsletter* (October, 1965).
[7] Robert L. Kent, "The Educational Scene: How to Evaluate," *Grade Teacher Magazine* (January, 1965).

tion, especially when dealing with early elementary school children.

For years, kindergarten teachers have been able to evaluate the children in their classes by close personal observations of their performance and interactions with their peers. Most kindergarten children are not yet capable of responding to written examinations involving reading and mathematical skills, but still the teacher is able to develop a complete and clear report of each student's progress.

In the final analysis, no one has ever discovered an infallible method of measuring the really important outcomes of a science program. Mere knowledge of content and facts that can be regurgitated on a written quiz is of relatively small value. The most important outcomes are the attitudes that students develop, the skills they gain, and the ability to operate and function satisfactorily under a set of different circumstances while using these same acquired skills and attitudes.

Evaluating a science program's effectiveness is very subjective and depends primarily on one's personal judgment. However, there are many subtle but significant signposts to look for. One might be the level of general interest, discussed earlier in this section. Another might be the number of pupils that volunteered for additional activities. How many youngsters carried on further experimentation at home or after school? How many slow readers turned to books for additional information? How much noticeable improvement has there been in the quality of work accomplished by individual students?

Do not attempt to judge or evaluate all students by the same criteria. Accept the individual differences of the students in the class and look for evidence of increased interest, effort, growth, and achievement.

> Leave the pupils mainly to their own spontaneous self-activities. The teacher may awaken and give direction to their curiosity by an occasional adroit question; but he should chiefly rely upon the action of his pupils' own powers for the discovery of new facts. As a general rule, nothing should be told to pupils which they can discover for themselves. The zealous and impatient teacher will often fail here, and the failure will be a serious and fatal one.
>
> It is so much easier to tell a child what we wish him to know, rather than wait for him to discover it for himself, that the inexperienced and careless can rarely resist the temptation but the babbling teacher will assuredly learn, in the long run the truth of the maxim, "The more haste, the worse speed."*

Maybe the message here is that we should **teach** less, evaluate carefully, and allow children to learn more.

### The Classroom

Classroom facilities and designs for teaching elementary school science vary greatly among school systems. With the present trend to include science as a major segment of the elementary school curriculum many schools have developed modern science rooms for this phase of the curriculum. Where these facilities are present they are usually found at the intermediate or the middle school level.

Most school systems are in the position of having to incorporate new science curricula within existing classroom space. Unfortunately, classroom design did not anticipate the degree of independent student involvement, with large amounts of material, now current in the **new science curricula**.

In general, schools have discovered that classroom size, limited storage facilities, and fixed classroom furniture now inhibit their progress in implementing new science curricula. To some degree it is difficult to understand how school planning (curriculum and building) permitted such a situation to develop. Schools have always maintained their interest in student involvement as well as independent and personalized development, yet fixed furniture and inadequate storage space seriously restrict attainment of these goals.

*26th Annual Report by the Superintendent of Public Instruction of the State of Michigan for the year, believe it or not, of *1862.*

30

Each elementary school classroom should have certain basic services available. These services are water, electricity, and bottled gas. Student desks (preferably tables) should be flat and not permanently fixed in the room. Peripheral counters, with storage space below, and large cabinets are needed for storage and work areas. These are the basic ingredients necessary in planning any classroom, not one in which the emphasis is only on science. There are many ways to incorporate these services and facilities into a classroom scheme that will permit flexible and imaginative teaching.

Lacking any portion or all of these basic requirements does not prohibit successful teaching but it does place a much greater burden on the classroom teacher.

With greater emphasis in science teaching on the independent use of materials by each child, the most important feature of a classroom must be its storage facilities and numerous flat **work surfaces** available for independent activities. Usually any room can be modified to permit greater storage and an increased amount of flat work surface area. The special room facilities—for example, special student desks and elaborate demonstration tables—can be very expensive and in large measure quite wasteful.

The elementary school classroom should be viewed as the place where learning can proceed realistically. The realism of our world and its **people to people** interaction is a culture in which technology, science, and the humanities coexist. Why not this same coexistence in our elementary school classrooms? Is it unrealistic to have a classroom design which with its simplicity and flexibility does permit as well as encourage co-existence of technology, science, and the humanities? Do specialized rooms further the child's understanding and appreciation of the necessary links among these three areas? The elementary school classroom needs to be specialized only to the extent that it provides for **the specialization** to be learning itself—learning in an atmosphere which combines experiences from technology, science, and the humanities. The elementary school which provides separate rooms for each specialized activity will find it very difficult to

implement such combined learning experiences. Certainly the complete absence of specialized facilities is as unreasonable as the presence of only specialized facilities. A balance between the two extremes is necessary.

Classrooms possessing the basic services (adequate storage and flat surface work areas) are ideally suited for all teaching. Science is not the only subject undergoing rapid changes in the classroom method of teaching. This is true in English, reading, mathematics, social studies and foreign languages. The emphasis is on greater independent use of numerous materials. More lasting results may be obtained by making these materials available in all rooms rather than available only in a series of specialized rooms.

The present trend toward ungraded schools places greater emphasis on the development of the individual child. Since the administrative structure of such a school needs to be flexible, large numbers of specialized classrooms would interfere with this desired flexibility. What we need in classroom design, school building planning, and curriculum development is less specialization in specific areas and greater specialization in our efforts to unify all learning experiences. The units described in this book lend themselves well to the ungraded school because they are composed of lessons in which students can progress at their own rate of speed.

## Concerning Science Equipment

When children are placed in a science environment and given the proper materials and direction, they can discover for themselves many of the fundamental concepts and principles which constitute the scientific process. This is science teaching by the inductive or laboratory method. It is one in which the child learns science in much the same manner that a scientist does, by actually doing.

Professor Jerome S. Bruner of Harvard cautions against arbitrary elimination of any scientific subject on the ground that it is unsuited to the elementary grades. In his book *The Process of Education* he says, "**Any subject can be taught effectively in some intellectually honest form to any child at any stage of development.**" His view is supported by Dr. Barbel Inhelder of the Rousseau Institute in Geneva, who on the basis of current experience with the learning process of children believes that basic notions in subjects such as physics are perfectly within the grasp of children of seven to ten years of age, provided that they are separated from mathematical expressions and studied through materials that the child can handle himself.

This in turn implies that at least in principle every student in a class should have his own equipment with which to work and experiment.

It is generally agreed that science in the elementary school should be based upon experience a child can gain by actively exploring with his senses. Obviously, then, equipment that a youngster can operate with his own hands is of prime importance.

Often science courses devote too much time in the laboratory absorbed in getting a right answer in the right blank on the right line—an answer that must agree with the one in the teacher's manual, all of which gives the student a false impression of the scientific endeavor. What we need are some experiments that have unexpected answers so the student will have an opportunity to develop some confidence in his own efforts and learn to account for his errors.

Max Planck, sometimes called the father of modern physics, when asked to name what he thought was the best laboratory manual, answered, "One hundred pages of blank paper." This is the spirit of the new laboratory approach where the student is given an opportunity to think, to organize his own ideas and to evaluate his findings in the light of known theory or thorough application. He will learn that the so-called conclusions only establish a basis for inquiry and as a mode of thinking provide the best means so far discovered to enable young people to participate in both the world of today and the world of tomorrow.[8]

The units in this book are built around relatively simple materials. Many of the supplies needed are available in supermarkets, dime stores, and hardware establishments at modest prices. Another place that may prove to be a great resource for teachers in gathering the necessary materials in sufficient quantities is the Federal Surplus Warehouses, which are located in each state. This agency permits educational and eleemosynary institutions to buy large amounts of valuable and useful materials at extremely low cost. In addi-

[8]Paul DeHart Hurd, Science Teaching for a Changing World, Scott Foresman, February, 1965.

tion, those curriculum development organizations that seem to be enjoying the most success have concentrated upon the wide use of simple and abundant materials. Commercial companies have also attempted to make large quantities of simple science apparatus marketable in economy packages. No longer, then, is it valid to exclude science from the elementary curriculum by complaining that equipment costs are prohibitive. The present emphasis on the use of equipment in the teaching of elementary school science assures the development of a wider choice of materials—games, puzzles, records, tapes, and single-concept film loops.

More significantly, the trend toward individualization of instruction and the need for classroom sets of certain items is causing: (1) simplification of present apparatus, (2) cost reduction of expensive items, and (3) creation of new apparatus of simple design. An example of a significant breakthrough was the development of simple microscopes which could be made available to large numbers of students at a very low cost. Hopefully, suitable planetaria, aquarea, transformers, meters, motors and numerous other items, will experience the same cost reduction. The expanded NDEA funds and other federal assistance are also reducing financial difficulty for school districts in purchasing equipment, library books, and related material.[9]

There is still another approach to solving the problem of equipment. Recently there has been a trend toward the development of science kits.

Today, as never before, there is a national concern to discover and develop abilities in science. In the elementary and secondary schools, there is a movement toward a sequential instructional program which would involve the offering of a laboratory science each year from kindergarten to high school graduation. But in some schools teachers are still handicapped by restricted space, inadequate facilities and equipment, short class periods and heavy work loads. Many have turned to science kits as a partial solution of their problems and are using them for such diverse purposes as demonstration, loans to pupils for home experimentation, aids to TV teaching, or for special projects such as science fairs and clubs. For some schools, the kit is the laboratory. A wide variety of kits for most science subjects at every grade level is available from commercial suppliers. The selection of kits presents special problems to teachers and school administrators who must judge their suitability for the school program.[10]

Science kits in themselves are no panacea for all problems involving school science equipment. Although packaged kits of many types are available for all grade levels and can prove very effective if utilized properly, their acceptance is by no means unanimous nor should it go completely unchallenged. For every proponent of science kits there is probably at least one dissenter. The critics of kits say that they may be of limited use, or unsuited to the school science program. Occasionally, the names assigned to some kits can be misleading. They may consist of mere collections of unrelated scientific novelties which contribute little to the understanding of basic concepts. The instruction manuals which accompany them may encourage **cookbook science** rather than promoting any interest in discovery. Sometimes the cost of a kit is higher than the total cost of the individual component parts, while replacement of parts may be a further problem, since some kits are rendered useless if certain key pieces are lost or broken. Often the quality of their construction may not measure up to standards for science equipment and the teacher and class may waste valuable time in the routine of re-sorting items after use.

[9]*Ibid.,* p. 15.

[10]Piltz, Albert and Gruver, William, *Science Equipment and Materials; Science Kits,* Office of Education Publication #29049.

On the other hand, the proponents of science kits claim that where science facilities are limited, kits make possible greater student participation in laboratory type activities. They make needed materials readily available in conveniently packaged form for teachers who generally have little time or training to prepare science demonstrations. Additionally, where storage space is at a premium, the compactness of kits is an asset. They can also provide an economical source of supplementary science material along with accessories at less cost than the same items purchased separately. On occasion, the wide use of kits may help meet the differing needs of pupils in the same class. Out of class, they can be used for data collecting by students at home during weekends and holidays. Interest in science may be stimulated by the use of kits and a poorly motivated student may become interested in experimenting by manipulation and assembling of materials in an investigation.

These two divergent views about science kits and their possible use in class are probably due to the vast differences to be found in the kits themselves. The kits vary widely in the range of their contents and their quality, value, aims, and degree of sophistication and adaptation to the rapidly changing demands of the science curriculum. The selection of kits is important and should be given careful consideration. The authors favor the wide use of simple materials, abundant and easily available locally.

Whatever a school's final decision is, if it results in more opportunities for the students to discover for themselves something about science, then the decision has been a wise one.

## Consultants and Science Specialists

In a recent survey compiled by the U. S. Office of Education concerned with science teaching in the elementary schools, two barriers to effective science teaching ranked highest.

First, the lack of adequate consultant service, and, second, the lack of supplies and equipment just discussed.

Consider the first requirement in the light of what is actually the general practice. Most elementary schools employ specialists to teach art, music, and physical education, while the area of science is left to be handled by the individual teacher. This survey points out that "**science is taught by a classroom teacher without the help of an elementary specialist in over 80 percent of the nation's public schools in grades one to five, and in over 70 percent of the schools in grades six to eight.**" Apparently, in spite of the recent new emphasis upon science in our schools since Sputnik, we are still doing little more than offering lip service in attempting to correct the situation. The demands placed upon the modern elementary school teacher to cover a multitude of subject areas and to teach them creates the need for help by specially trained personnel.

What is the role of the science specialist or supervisor? In too many schools where a specialist is employed he has evolved into another administrator charged with the responsibility of watching over a teacher's shoulder and writing up a report to be added to his dossier when he is considered for a new contract. This kind of supervision is probably worse than none. What most elementary teachers really want is a resource person—someone who has had training in the sciences and has had experience working with both elementary school teachers and children.

This individual must be extremely patient and be willing to rush to a teacher or school in need of help at a moment's notice. He can generally be seen hurrying from one school to another, automobile and suit pockets flowing over with sundry kinds of science materials and an eager look of anticipation on his face.

The science specialist has to be a sort of jack-of-all-trades in that on occasion he might have act-

ually to instruct an elementary class or assist the teacher in introducing a new unit. He may have to fix a broken piece of apparatus or rescue a frightened teacher from some **wild animal** brought in by a student. An example of an unusual request follows:

Dear Mr. Science Supervisor,

Birth—a baby pigeon during night. Another on the way.

If you have a large medicine dropper Mrs. Z. could use it.

School Secretary

Most important of all, he is available for consultation with both teacher and student and is ready to offer advice and assistance whenever needed. Teachers trying out new approaches in science need someone to talk with them who has more than a cursory knowledge about the subject and who is not reluctant to offer a bit of constructive criticism or a pat on the back for a job well done. Many courageous teachers have attempted to achieve new horizons in their classrooms but lose their initiative for lack of having another adult who genuinely cares sharing this interest.

To provide a full-time science consultant is to ask for something more than the occasional help that is available from the state departments or from an interested science person at the high school or a local resource person in the community. This is a job which is full-time and is very demanding in its diversification of roles. The elementary science specialist, science coordinator, supervisor of science, or whatever the title may be,

is responsible for conducting in-service workshops for teachers. In addition he serves as the spearhead of new curriculum development and oversees the science budget, checks on all equipment to make sure that it is operable, instructs the teachers in its use, heads committees for purchase of books and supplies, and so on.

The key to effective science teaching in the elementary school lies ultimately with the classroom teacher, but he must have the necessary help that can best be rendered only by a science specialist on call when that help is most needed.

To summarize: in the past more emphasis was placed upon the information and content aspects of elementary school science than on the performance or investigative process of science. Now new and exciting programs giving children a feeling for science through active involvement are beginning to flourish. The authors believe there ought to be many opportunities for children to make mistakes. By doing so, children learn much about the nature of scientific inquiry. Teachers should not be disappointed by a child's failure in an activity or experiment to obtain meaningful results in the traditional sense. What the child has found out about the techniques for conducting an investigation can be of great value. A child's understanding cannot be furthered by just talking to him. Children must be presented with situations in which they experiment—try things, manipulate symbols, form questions, and compare results with other children.

In the units and lessons delineated in this book young children are given the opportunity to practice designing equipment, devising techniques for experimentation, measuring, keeping records of their results, and analyzing the data that is collected.

# Why Do It This Way?

# Why Do It This Way?

## Designing Science Units

Designing a science unit at any level requires more attention to how children learn than dedication to how many facts can be conveyed. The primary child's self-expression is largely uninhibited, his activity is essential and his attention span radically changes with time. He intuitively explores his environment indifferent to society's restrictions. Curiosity results either from wanting to find an answer or just wanting to find out. The motivation is generally wanting to find out—to find out an object's shape or color, to feel things, smell things, taste things, hear unusual noises, make his own sounds, and above all to participate.

In large measure the primary school teacher's main objective is communication of ideas and concepts. Primary children are capable of learning scientific concepts because there are so many which can be illustrated by experiments in which only one or two interactions of objects is observed. The child can express himself by pictures or actions long before he has attained any proficiency in reading or writing.

## Learning Through Our Senses

All information is gained through our senses. The early beginnings of understanding about the surrounding environment should receive special attention through activities which will improve or develop:

1. Observation of objects with the senses
2. Observation of interaction of objects
3. Classification of observations—similarities, differences, and changes.

Professor Bruner has emphasized that there are two kinds of learning behavior. One is clear,

meaningful, rational, deductive, purposeful, and straightforward whereas the other is hypothetical, tentative, intuitive, playful, imaginative, and sometimes even wrong.

During the elementary years the latter behavior—playful, hypothetical, intuitive, tentative—ought to be emphasized, building a foundation for later years on which clear, meaningful, rational, deductive learning can proceed.

The development of classification skills permits a wide range of activities and considerable self-expression by children. Objects or things are big, small, hot, cold, pretty, round, funny, sharp, noisy—these and many others are descriptive words commonly used by children to classify objects and/or people in their environment. As teachers we can skillfully structure class activities which encourage active development of each child's observational and classification skills. However, we should be cautioned that all learning has not or will not take place in the classroom. More than we dare imagine goes on outside the school. Therefore, start activities in the class assuming that many skills are already a part of the child's experience. You frequently will be surprised!

In all classification or sorting activities be sure to include the process of counting—ask how many are there in a pile or in a certain classification. Have the children write the number, or reproduce the objects by drawing the number of circles, squares, beads, etc., on construction paper. The reason for this is not so much for recording skills, but to link motor skills with classification activities, hence permitting the hands to practice drawing what the mind *sees*. This can be accomplished by exactly duplicating the classified objects by a drawing in conjunction with using the **shorthand** of writing numbers. Activities of this nature become the vehicles through which children grow in general physical and mental development, the use of words and the exercise of self-expression being of paramount importance. The **final test** for the acquisition of many of these classification skills will likely not be apparent in the primary grades. Several years of accumulated raw experience will reveal results at the intermediate and middle school levels.

By the time a youngster is in kindergarten he is capable of imagining his environment other than as he perceives it. The primary level is the **preoperational stage**, as labeled by Piaget. The youngster usually makes judgments in terms of how things look. He will have difficulty in coordinating variables or realizing that objects can possess more than one property—for example, the properties of shape, size, or weight associated with the collection of blocks discussed in the How to Begin section. He can deal with the rudiments of classification and the beginning notions of series (arrangement in separate sets of all the cubes, spheres, rectangles, etc.). Therefore, implement learning activities which take advantage of these early skills and attempt to nourish their development.

Early learning experiences in science need not be complicated. In fact, these experiences should not be labeled **science experiences,** for they require the youngsters to develop and practice skills unique to the total development of a child—not just unique to one field of learning. Units the teacher will develop must take advantage of existing materials and in most instances these materials should be available in large quantities. Frequently, teacher-designed or commercially designed units are undertaken using insufficient quantities of the required materials. The major key to the successful completion of a child-centered activity is the presence of adequate quantities of the necessary materials. There can be no short cuts on materials: if units call for clay, soap, marbles, buttons, magnifying glasses, light sources, etc., insure they are available in sufficient quantity before the unit is commenced. Remember, there is a vast assortment of common household materials which can serve as the equipment and supplies necessary for the development of a science unit. For primary children, objects, material, and **things** should be large in size. This may not be as necessary for upper primary children as it is for kindergarten and first grade children.

## Testing a Unit

Evaluation is an integral part of science teaching. It may be built into some units, while others do not lend themselves to direct evaluation. There is no fixed requirement for direct evaluation. Most of the learning activities at the primary level are basic to all learning, and it is possible to evaluate progress not only by the amount of information retained but by the manner of acceptance and the approach to new situations in other fields. Probably the best evaluation of a particular activity is an interested class, for an interested class is a successful one.

As primary children these youngsters encounter their first formalized experiences in spelling, arithmetic, reading, science, and several other areas. All want to be successful or at least adequate to the task. A child's view of his own adequacy changes continually, the changes being directly related to his own day-to-day attitudes and the behavior of others toward him. To help him cope with this continually changing viewpoint of his inherent adequacy it is important to show him he is capable of learning through experience. Furthermore, he needs to recognize that he has learned, has really made progress.

However, some problems children may confront will not be solvable. Some problems turn out to be too difficult. Yet failure to solve them does not mean a child is inadequate, instead it may mean he has had little opportunity in independent problem solving situations.

Creating situations in which children are encouraged to express their own ideas—many of which may be wrong—and then continually correcting them may lead them to think that all their ideas are wrong. Even though their ideas may be incorrect, children should be encouraged to think and find out that they are able to do so. Not all their misconceptions can be corrected without impeding the child's desire or search for adequacy.

In order to strengthen the child's viewpoint of his own adequacy we must permit him to do those things he does well for longer periods of time. Is it wrong for a child to enjoy his own ability at a specific task? Why must he quickly move to another immediately after achieving a success?

Realization that he can learn through experience, recognition of his own progress, acceptance of the notion that some problems will be insolvable, and knowledge that he is free to express his ideas— these are some of the major attitudes we want

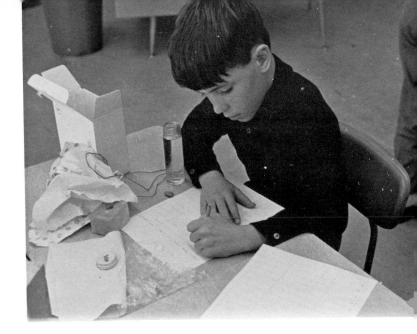

every child to develop. It is at the primary level that we must begin to make his attitudes meaningful in assisting the development of his feeling of adequacy.

## How Primary Children Communicate

Primary children are in the early stages of establishing some sort of structure for their thinking patterns, beginning to realize that language (communication) is important, and eager to communicate about what they are doing or have seen. As classroom activities develop and expand, more children want to communicate about their experiences. Young children will listen to each other provided the teacher gives them the opportunity. Must all communication always be between the child and teacher? The clever teacher can develop a classroom discussion, **among children**. For this discussion to be significant the experience discussed must first be significant to the children and each child's involvement in this experience must overlap with or be related to others in a meaningful way.

The initial impressions that a primary teacher makes on children will significantly affect their future development and attitude toward learning and communicating.

Early childhood learning is spontaneous and not necessarily sequential. It cannot always be structured. Language skills come into existence after physical movement and contact with **things** have

served to inform the youngster of his surroundings. Body movement and physical contact with objects introduces him to, as well as maintains, his interest in the living community. Experience molds his awareness of the many existing relationships. He measures, compares, groups, matches, feels, smells, tastes, sees, hears, and instinctively employs his body in rhythmic patterns, reacting to various musical tones and beats. He is serious and intensely personal about his involvement in all physical activity. Fantasy, spontaneity, curiosity, enthusiasm—all play their part. The accumulation of knowledge gained from play and other experience becomes the basis of the child's early understanding of relationships and abstract ideas or concepts. Children must be encouraged to react with and change conditions of their environment. Such activity develops as the teacher takes a more positive role in structuring some of the child's activities. Language becomes more important; symbolic representations become acceptable and mental operations more precise. For primary children words are not the only means of communication. They will express themselves through the language of music, rhythm, art, and dancing. These activities require combined physical and mental coordination. Each activity is a means of self-expression for children. Learning results from children attempting to express themselves and all forms of expression are equally important. These forms of expression should be utilized in the teaching of science.

Primary children require both mental and physical development. Physical development means coordinated bodies capable of motor and manipulative skills. They must have equipment that encourages experimentation: building blocks, springs, moving things, balances, pulleys, measuring devices, and magnifying glasses. School begins to assume the character of a place, not so much where rote drills and rules predominate, but a place in which children learn to operate creatively and purposefully in a group. Children cannot be forced into group activities, and ways must be devised to bring them into contact rapidly and in a natural way.

Primary children are especially interested in their own and others' physical features—hair, skin, shape, size—all the features which make up an individual. Classroom activities should capitalize on this natural interest. One approach is to insert in the primary curriculum specifically designed units to consider the human body. Some school systems refer to this as the health curriculum, and it is completed in graduated steps throughout the elementary and secondary school levels. It may validly be asked, however, why the study of the human body, health, proper nourishment, and family relationships needs to be a separate topic. It is more realistic and significant as an integral part of all classroom activities.

### Discovering the Rules of the Game

Primary children are usually quite uninhibited by the **rules** of accepted adult behavior. They will freely discuss family events: "Mommy and Daddy had a fight"; "We are going to have a baby"; "I didn't take a bath last night, it's been almost three days"; "We had ginger ale and cookies for lunch"; "Mommy got a baby last night"; "My grandmother died of an attack"; "We had a big party last night with lots of noise"; "Mommy's teeth came out." Unsolicited comments of this sort are numerous. Primary children are very open in their statements about themselves and their relationships to other people in their environment. The suggested science units in this book encourage continued identification of the **physical self** and its relationships to people and things in the environment. Family relationships, body shape or size, sex (male or female), reproduction, proper

nourishment, and hygiene habits are part of the real world and should be an integral part of a child's history, English, art, mathematics, and science experiences. At the primary level all living things—guppies, earthworms, molds, embryos—stimulate interest in these topics. Animal relationships, body size and shape, sex, reproduction, nourishment, and cleanliness should be related to people. Primary children are eager to make comparisons and to relate their observations of living animals to real people. Discussion stimulated by comparisons of observations of animals and of people should result in learning experiences more meaningful than those confined to a particular health and family living curriculum.

Primary children are ready to try anything. They have the right blend of curiosity, imagination, physical stamina, and spontaneous motivation to make learning effective. This period in a youngster's life passes by quickly. If our classroom materials and our classroom teachers are not ready for the challenges these characteristics present, the most impressionable years of childhood have been lost.

# How to Do It

# How to Do It

Teaching is not synonymous with telling. The teacher is not primarily a guardian of the archives; he is first a guide to children, assuring them of their right to full development of their gifts. He knows this development is not always easy to assure; for children do not choose their parents, nor their society.[11]

The teacher creates the atmosphere in which children react with their environment in a personalized manner. The method of science is not one but many, for different people possess different ways of approaching problems. Science assumes an open mind and a readiness to question or modify beliefs on the basis of evidence. Therefore, the successful teacher must possess certain unique qualities. He is a person who listens to ideas, helps children find exciting things to do, encourages students to work independently, doesn't tell all the answers but **permits** mistakes, is excited about student ideas, stimulates question formation and helps students realize that they have learned. The teacher must realize that it is primarily through a youngster's school experiences that he comes to view himself as an able person—able to think, work cooperatively with others, and to learn new things.

During the primary years, the school system is attempting to **set its mold** for each inquisitive, active, noisy, and frequently annoying little **creature.** Youngsters are told when to talk, when to be

quiet, when to take out their work materials, when to put them away, when to go to the lavatory, when it is time for a drink, when to say good morning if the principal or another visitor enters the room—and so it goes with each phase of the school day becoming a regimented pattern forming the parts which make up what we adults designate the **system.** The important thing seems to be the **system** and conformity to its rules of accepted behavior. Schools have become very successful at teaching children conventional responses.

Teachers, in their efforts to meet the standards established by the **system,** unknowingly permit the regimentation of the **system** to flavor their classroom activities. We do an excellent job of taking a heterogeneous group of youngsters as they enter school and over a period of years blend them into one large homogenized mass and proudly acclaim them educated. All we need to do next is to figure out some way of pasturizing the resultant product and the process would be completed. Youngsters are individuals and we must make every effort to treat them as such if true learning is to be fostered.

The following units represent doing activities which will enable the teacher to facilitate learning. The materials required are simple and should be available in sufficient quantity before starting. Not all of the units require the same period of time. They are all open-ended and require considerable teacher planning. Some of the units are much

[11]Paul F. Brandwein, Elements in a Strategy for Teaching Science in the Elementary Schools, Harcourt, Brace & World.

longer than others and may at first appear to be too lengthy for primary children. For some classes this may be true and therefore it may be possible to complete only a portion of a particular unit. A unit may be ended prematurely and continued later in the year or possibly not at all. These units are designed to permit maximum flexibility by the teacher in planning classroom activities. The major considerations are student interest and active involvement. Provided a particular unit continues to generate interest, enthusiasm, and active involvement, it would seem appropriate to continue and/or expand the scope of the unit. Certainly it is imperative that the teacher generate personal interest and enthusiasm for the type of student-centered activities advocated by these units. The teacher must indicate by his actions his interest and enthusiasm in each one of the activities. The units provide the teacher with concepts, activities, and necessary background material; imagination, initiative, patience, and understanding must be provided by the teacher. None of these units should be considered strictly science units but rather experiences which will permit youngsters to react with their environment and by so doing gain practice in thinking, relating, observing, expressing, and cooperating.

Hopefully, some of the experiences in these units will motivate the classroom teacher to develop additional units. Remember, the primary objective of teaching is not merely the imparting of facts and laws to children. We should want our children to improve in the skills of thinking, observing, relating, and working independently. In order for children to acquire these skills time must be devoted to the practice of them. Science can be used as a **vehicle** to encourage and carry on these activities, probably at the expense of **not** covering all the **must areas**, but with the possible reward being youngsters better prepared to read, talk, and think with understanding. This then is the prime responsibility of a teacher.

Children require confrontation with real things and real problems, not solely to increase their storehouse of factual information but to have frequent opportunity to exercise and improve their skills in observing, relating, expressing, and thinking. Dedication to the teaching of science implies dedication to the task of helping children to learn—and the learning experience should encompass **all** experiences interrelated into a unique **oneness**. The techniques employed in making science exciting and meaningful to young children are the same techniques needed to make English, reading, spelling, mathematics, history, and art exciting and meaningful. As teachers, our efforts should be aimed at creating the classroom atmosphere in which this **oneness** becomes a reality.

# BALANCING BLOCKS

### How to Begin

Primary children enjoy comparing things. They compare size, color, and shape, and in this unit they will compare the effects of objects positioned on a board which is balanced on a fulcrum.

Children can gain understanding of how objects are balanced through a series of confrontations in which blocks, a fulcrum, and a board become the materials with which first-hand experience is accumulated. Therefore, the essential ingredients for each child are a board (plywood ½" x 3" x 24"); a fulcrum (closet pole, 1½" diameter cut in half and 4" long) and eight blocks (1" x 1" x 1"). These items can be made commercially or supplied through the school's industrial arts department. The board should be ruled off in equal divisions. Use a Magic Marker. First draw a straight line across the middle of the board and then make similar marks every 2 inches on either side of the middle. Label the marks on either side of the middle 1, 2, 3 . . . The middle mark should not have a label. As an optional approach you might wish to use a board 40 inches long with ten blocks to relate to the base ten number system.

### Why Do It This Way?

The simple materials this unit requires will expose children to countless experiences in which they control their involvement in an experimental situation. The facts connected with this unit could be conveyed in one or two lessons, yet if accomplished in this manner it could hardly be labeled science teaching. Science teaching implies much more than just learning facts. More importantly, it means giving children a chance to make mistakes, to "cut and try" and to develop confidence which is not controlled primarily by teacher approval. Therefore, in this unit be patient: give children the opportunity to gain experience in the bal-

ancing situation, and by so doing accomplish in a long time what you may feel could be done in considerably less time.

### How to Do It

The activities for this unit can center around written question sheets developed by the teacher or verbal questions periodically stated by the teacher. Children will want to record their findings. Any scheme which is meaningful to the child should be accepted. After the unit is in full progress you can have the children share their various recording methods. Possibly the class will then decide on a common procedure.

Give a board and fulcrum to each child and state the following question: "Can you balance the board on the fulcrum?" The children will perform this task in several ways. The board can be placed flat on the fulcrum, on edge, or on one of its ends. Control your desire to show them how you think it should be done. You asked a question which by its very nature implies individual responses. Must these responses all agree with your preconceived notion of how to balance the board? Most children will balance the board flat on the fulcrum and some on its edge (very few will do it on its end). Once the blocks are introduced generally the children will balance the board flat on the fulcrum.

Hand out the blocks—eight to each child—and then let the children "play." For convenience in handling and passing out material place in separate plastic bags the eight blocks for each child.

Now starts the series of encounters in which children gain experience with the balancing board and blocks. Use the following questions to guide their involvement. The questions gradually become more difficult. Each question will require varying degrees of time and practice for each child. Do not keep the children in "lock step." You can develop written lesson sheets using the following questions. A note of caution: it is better to have each child work for a short time (thirty to thirty-five minutes) two or three times a week on these questions rather than attempt to rush through them in a few prolonged periods. Give time for reflection on things outside the classroom; given

time, children will observe applications of the board and fulcrum outside the class.

## Questions

1. Balance the board on the fulcrum. Place two blocks over the fulcrum. Is the board still in balance? Where else can you place two blocks and still keep the board in balance? Record as many answers as you can.

2. Balance the board on the fulcrum. Place two blocks on one side of the fulcrum. Can you balance the board with two more blocks? How many different ways can you balance two blocks on one side of the fulcrum?

3. Balance the board on the fulcrum. Place three blocks on one side of the fulcrum. Can you balance the board with three more blocks? How many different ways can you balance three blocks on one side of the fulcrum with three blocks on the other side of the fulcrum?

4. Balance the board on the fulcrum. Place four blocks on one side of the fulcrum. Can you balance the board with four more blocks? How many different ways can you balance four blocks on one side of the fulcrum with four blocks on the other side of the fulcrum?

5. Balance the board on the fulcrum. Place two blocks on one side of the fulcrum. .Can you balance the board with one block on the other side of the fulcrum? How many different ways can you balance two blocks on one side of the fulcrum with one block on the other side of the fulcrum?

6. Balance the board on the fulcrum. Place three blocks on one side of the fulcrum. Can you balance the board with one block on the other side of the fulcrum? How many different ways can you balance three blocks on one side of the fulcrum with one block on the other side of the fulcrum?

7. Balance the board on the fulcrum. Place three blocks on one side of the fulcrum. Can you balance the board with two blocks on the other side of the fulcrum? How many differ-

ent ways can you balance three blocks on one side of the fulcrum with two blocks on the other side of the fulcrum?

8. (a) Balance the board on the fulcrum. Place three blocks on position three on one side of the fulcrum. What would you do to balance these blocks? Write down some of the answers you get.

(b) Balance the board on the fulcrum. Place four blocks on position four on one side of the fulcrum. What would you do to balance these blocks? Write down some of the answers you get.

(c) Balance the board on the fulcrum. Spread four blocks out at different places on one side of the fulcrum. What would you do to balance these blocks? Write down some of the answers you get.

9. If one block was placed at position two on one side of the fulcrum, *guess* where you would place one block on the other side of the fulcrum. Write down your guess. Try it and see if your guess was correct.

10. If two blocks were placed at position three on one side of the fulcrum, *guess* where you would place two blocks on the other side of the fulcrum. Write down your guess. Try it and see if your guess was correct.

11. If three blocks were placed at position four on one side of the fulcrum, *guess* where you would place three blocks on the other side of the fulcrum. Write down your guess. Try it and see if your guess was correct.

12. If one block was placed at position four on one side of the fulcrum, *guess* where you would place two blocks on the other side of the fulcrum. Write down your guess. Try it and see if your guess was correct.

13. If two blocks were placed at position three on one side of the fulcrum, *guess* where you would place three blocks on the other side of the fulcrum. Write down your guess. Try it and see if your guess was correct.

14. Guess where you must place two blocks on one side of the fulcrum to balance three blocks out two spaces on the other side of the fulcrum.

15. Guess where you must place four blocks on one side of the fulcrum to balance four blocks out five spaces on the other side of the fulcrum.

16. Balance the board on the fulcrum. Move the board to the right or left until the fulcrum is under position one on the board. Can you balance the board when it is like this? Can you balance the board when the fulcrum is under position two on the board?

17. You have been balancing the board in many different ways; sometimes you used the same number of blocks on each side of the fulcrum and sometimes you did not. Can you think of a general rule for balancing the board with the blocks? First try to make a general rule for the times you used the same number of blocks on each side of the fulcrum. Will your rule work for the case when there are a different number of blocks on each side of the fulcrum?

Questions 1 through 7 provide specific directions as to the number of blocks necessary for each experience. Initially the children will experiment with the same number of blocks on each side of the fulcrum (questions 2–4) while later they will experiment with different numbers of blocks on either side of the fulcrum (questions 5–7). Encourage the children to obtain many responses to each question. Their answers can be recorded on a worksheet which has drawings of the board and fulcrum, for example:

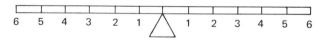

The children will try to hurry through the questions, for they have probably always equated number of questions answered with success—a good grade. Slow the children down by getting them to try several different balancing combinations (recording each) for each question.

The children are gaining experience with the "balancing situation" during the early questions (1-7). The teacher's role is to create an atmosphere that will permit this independent investigation. Do not try to direct it.

Question 8 presents some problems in a different way. No mention is made of the number of blocks which should be used to get the board in balance. In all previous questions the number of blocks to be used was indicated. Initially this will confuse the children. Do not be too eager to render assistance or explain.

Questions 9-15 ask the children to make "guesses." Basically, these questions are trying to determine if the children can use the collection of experience gained from earlier questions.

Observe the children closely. If a child makes a guess which does not result in the board remaining in balance, watch very closely what he does to correct the situation. For example, in question 10, if the child places two blocks on position two, the board will not balance. The important reaction to observe is what this child does to correct the situation. Does he immediately move these blocks out farther from the fulcrum without any hesitation? Does he seem confused or uncertain as to what direction to move the blocks to attain balance? If there is no hesitation in moving the blocks out farther, this probably indicates that past experience in earlier questions has been meaningful. If the child is uncertain, as revealed by his actions, this could mean he has not gained enough experience in the "balancing situation."

In question 16 it is suggested that the balancing problem be tried when the fulcrum is not directly under the midpoint. This may seem difficult for some children.

It is important to give each child an opportunity to develop a "balancing rule" as requested in question 17. Very few can develop a quantitative rule but most can express a qualitative rule; for example: a few blocks placed far from the fulcrum can balance several blocks placed close to the fulcrum. Some children may notice that when the same number of blocks are used on each side of the fulcrum they are always positioned on the same number. The "balancing rule" is a multiplication rule:

the sum of the multiplication of each block times its respective distance from the fulcrum on one side of the fulcrum must be equal to the same sum on the other side of the fulcrum. For example:

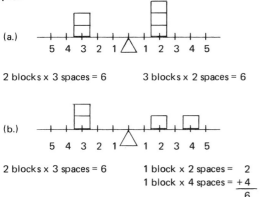

(a.)

    5  4  3  2  1  △  1  2  3  4  5

2 blocks x 3 spaces = 6        3 blocks x 2 spaces = 6

(b.)

    5  4  3  2  1  △  1  2  3  4  5

2 blocks x 3 spaces = 6        1 block x 2 spaces =    2
                               1 block x 4 spaces = + 4
                                                      6

Very few primary children will develop this quantitative rule, but they *all* can work at developing some qualitative rule which indicates their general understanding of the "balancing situation."

High interest can be generated in this unit. After completion of the work with the boards you may be able to obtain one large plank (12' long) and a block of wood (to serve as a fulcrum) and try some of the questions using children as the "blocks."

Some children may talk about machines that act like the balancing board. This could be an easy way to move into discussions about simple machines. Some teachers have discovered ways of using the "marked balancing board" as a number line in their arithmetic work.

"Balancing Blocks" will present many opportunities for all forms of child-centered expression.

# BUBBLES

### How to Begin

From birth, human beings learn primarily through sensory perception. The primary child is an excellent example. He has had approximately five and one half to seven and one half years of experience but has amassed a great deal of knowledge in this comparatively short span of time.

He has begun to interpret sounds and manipulate them reasonably well in forming communicable sentences. He can coordinate his feet, legs, and body for walking, maneuver fingers and hands for grasping and fetching, and has learned how to use tears and smiles to advantage.

Somehow he even learned to keep away from

danger—but not always. Many kinds of things may be learned through direct experiences, some painful and some pleasurable.

Blowing soap bubbles is a rather simple activity through which young children can learn some fundamentals of science and have fun in the process. Obtain some liquid detergent, straws, small paper cups, sponges (for clean up), and an ample supply of old newspapers (desk covering).

## Why Do It This Way?

The young child is endowed with so much natural curiosity that even a parent's chiding and reprimands may not always deter the instinctive desire to explore, to search, to smell, to touch, to taste, to listen, and to observe.

This simple unit deals with the innate inquisitiveness of young children and provides many opportunities to develop and sharpen these skills. It should be started with the idea that learning can be fun, which could very well be considered an end in itself. From this premise the children and teacher may discover together some of the wonders of science without necessarily having a predetermined goal. This is particularly important at an early age, when we should be concerned more with developing skills and an approach to investigation, than with concrete results or conclusions.

## How to Do It

Due to the short attention span of the average primary child and the unplanned interruptions or detours which probably will occur, there is not a set time limit for this unit. It may be stopped at any point and resumed in the "as near as possible future." It might be better to close a lesson session or stop the activity while the interest is still high. This might be about twenty minutes for kindergarten children, but the teacher should use her own judgment. The titles of the various lessons are for convenience only and the activities need not be presented as separate lessons. Each lesson is presented in dialogue form.

Prepare one half a cup of liquid detergent for each child. Cut the straws into thirds. Provide each child with a straw, three sheets of drawing paper, and crayons. Cover the desks with newspaper and have sponges available in case of spilling. Play a recording of "I'm Forever Blowing Bubbles" (Lawrence Welk). Have helpers pass out only the cups of detergent and the crayons.

*Lesson 1*   Do liquids pour? What about solids?

Teacher:   What do I have in my hand, Tommy? [a cake of soap] Jane, how is it the same or different from what you have in your nutcup? Jerry, come here and

56

pour this cake of soap into this cup. Can you do it? Sara, bring your cup here and pour its contents into this cup. [You could expand this concept by asking more children to attempt to pour various things—*i.e.,* blocks, juice, crayons, water, etc.]

Teacher: Yes, we can pour what we have in our cups. We have a liquid in our cups. Here is the way that word looks. [Write "liquid" on the board.] Let's all read it: liquid.

Teacher: Mary, what do you suppose our liquid is? Johnny? Bill? Cindy? How does our liquid smell, Tina? What does our liquid feel like, Craig? How does our liquid look, Frank? Does our liquid make sounds?

Children: [All will be feeling, smelling, and tasting the liquid. Probably someone will discover and answer, "It's detergent." If not, give hints and try to draw it out of the children. Refrain from giving away the answer. "Detergent" has become a fairly common household term as a result of television commercials and may be offered as a solution by a number of children.]

*Lesson 2* Understanding of the word "sphere."

Teacher: What might we do with our liquid detergent, Phyllis? Johnny and Rita, would you please give each person one of these pieces of straw? What shape do you think you will make when you blow through your straw, Kenny? Dip one end of your straw into your liquid detergent. Let it drip once, then hold it up and blow. [While children are blowing bubbles the teacher may pass out paper to each child. Permit time to play with the bubbles.]

Teacher: Draw on your paper the shape of your bubbles. [While the children draw, the

teacher may walk around getting individual explanations of the bubbles. Time permitting, the children's "stories" are a valuable way in which children may interpret what is happening. Each child may hold up his interpretation and tell a story about it if he so desires. Bring out use of the word "sphere." Write it on the board and let all "read" it. You may attempt some reading readiness with attention focused on the sounds in words like "liquid," "sphere," "detergent," by emphasizing the beginning sounds of each.]

*Lesson 3*  Air can move.

Teacher:  What makes your bubble move? How does it move? You have a liquid in your cup. Now at the end of your straw you have a bubble. Where did it come from? Are all your bubbles the same size? Why?

*Lesson 4*  Have children hold bubbles in the path of sunrays coming in the window.

Teacher:  What color is your detergent? What happens? [Have helpers pass a piece of white paper to each child.]

Teacher:  Using your crayons, make the colors of your soap bubbles. What happens to your bubbles? Why do you think this happens? Do your bubbles make any sounds? Where do they go? After they pop what do you see on the newspaper on the table, or on the floor? Why did the drop of liquid fall? Why are there sometimes no drops of liquid on the floor? If we left the drop on the paper, what would happen to it? Let's try one. [Have helpers pass a piece of paper to each child.] Blow a bubble and let it pop on your paper. Use a crayon to draw around your drop of liquid. Put your name on it or a special mark so you'll know which is yours. Put your paper with the drop of liquid on the shelf in back of the room. We shall look at them tomorrow.

*Lesson 5*  Dancing like bubbles.

Teacher:  The bubbles you made were lovely. Remember how lightly they moved. Did they make any sounds? Let's be bubbles and float gently through the air. [Turn on the record player and dance with the children.]

The questions suggested for the teacher may be varied. Questions and the subsequent answers will determine how this unit progresses. A discussion of variables involved in blowing bubbles will develop and lead to new observations as the children's natural curiosity has been awakened. The bubbles are the "means" of getting children stimulated to make observations and discuss them with you and the rest of the class.

The following is a list of general areas for further investigation, skills, and concepts which can result from this unit, and brief information concerning the phenomenon of bubbles.

1. Liquids, solids, and various kinds and states of matter.
2. How we discover through our senses.
3. Helping to develop habits of observing closely, thinking deductively, predicting, making inferences, and recording findings.
4. A fundamental understanding of shapes, particularly the characteristics.
5. Air is always moving. Bubbles move on the air.
6. Air from inside you fills the bubble.
7. Light rays can be broken up by bubbles and appear rainbow-colored.
8. Some simple generalizations concerning density as bubbles move through the air and some idea about evaporation as bubbles disappear.
9. The outside of a liquid acts as if it were an elastic skin.
10. The elastic film tends to become as small as it can and takes the form which has the smallest surface for its content, *i.e.,* the sphere.
11. Air inside the elastic skin will get out if it can.
12. If commercial detergents aren't available, a good solution may be made of castile soap, pure glycerine, and pure distilled water. (Commercial detergents usually contain some glycerine.)
13. Bubbles can be made to change shape, to slip inside one another, to blow out candles, with proper equipment and solutions.

# BUTTONS, BEADS, AND "THINGS"

### How to Begin

Many different materials should be collected in preparation for this unit. They should be collected in large quantities in order to permit simultaneous use by all children. Suggested items to obtain are listed below:

marbles
wooden blocks—all sizes
rubber stoppers
cork stoppers
buttons—four different sizes
flat washers, different sizes
nuts and bolts
magnifying lenses
any other assortment of items obtainable in large quantities

As the children deal with the objects in this unit it is your purpose to encourage discussion of the physical properties of these objects. In preparing for this unit the hardware store, the attic, or cellar will be great sources from which to supply your class with a vast assortment of objects. Your imagination can expand the suggested list tenfold. The children can assist in gathering these objects.

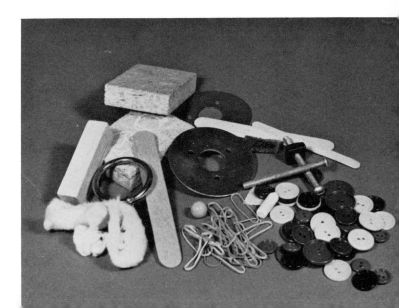

## Why Do It This Way?

In this unit the major goal is to direct the attention of the children to the properties of various objects and show how these properties can be used as guides in differentiating between objects.

In dealing with objects the tendency of most children and adults is to first concern themselves with the function of a particular object. If a child is given an object he recognizes, his first reaction is to tell what he knows it can do. If a child is given an object he does not recognize, his first reaction is to consider how it can be used. In this unit it is hoped children can be encouraged to discuss the **properties** of objects and not their **function.** Certainly function will be part of the discussions but the teacher's aim should be to redirect attention to the properties of objects.

In learning about and discussing the properties of many different objects, eventually all the "senses" will come into play. Feeling, smelling, hearing, and tasting are all activities of extreme interest to the primary youngster.

In this unit a common problem is the teacher's eagerness to get on with another activity—possibly fearing that boredom may dampen some of the enthusiasm if the same activity lasts too long. Take this chance; children are surprisingly self-sufficient and we too often interpret aimless play with materials as being pointless. It is hard to say when the play is really aimless and when it is not. Ideas, expressions, and responses don't always occur

when we want them to—why would they?

## How to Do It

The various activities suggested for this unit have been divided into lessons. This does not imply that each lesson is one class period. Most lessons will require several class periods. Set aside two or three thirty-minute periods each week to consider the activities in this unit. These periods should not be on consecutive days.

### Lesson 1

In the first lesson try to get the children to talk about objects in the room. The teacher can initiate this discussion by saying that she is "thinking of an object in the back of the room which is blue." The children then attempt to guess what the object is. Various children can be called on to give their clue for some object in the room. This kind of activity will focus attention on the properties (color, shape, size, etc.) of objects. The function of some of the objects selected will undoubtedly come into the discussion. This is to be expected and should not be considered "wrong." The role of the teacher is to focus class attention on the properties rather than the use.

### Lesson 2

In this lesson each youngster should receive a box (cigar box suggested) containing an assortment of objects. Each box can contain chalk, crayons, marbles, blocks, rubber bands, etc. Caution the children not to look inside their boxes when they receive them. You will not be able to contain their curiosity for long, but ask them to shake the boxes and tell you what they think is inside.

At this point have them open the boxes and direct each child to select an object from the box. Ask several youngsters to tell about the object they have selected—the properties of that object. Write down these properties on the board or on a chart. It probably will be necessary to start a "properties word chart" which will aid children in describing the properties of objects. As the children describe the objects they select, develop

60

an extensive word chart.

After the children seem to have the ability to describe objects by their properties, try a simple sorting exercise. One way to start this is to suggest that everyone remove from the box all objects that are shiny (or rough, soft, smooth, etc.). Various exercises similar to this can be tried. Do not be concerned if some children have difficulty in categorizing objects by properties. This is difficult for many children. Later lessons will assist them in this approach.

### Lesson 3

In this lesson, and in those to follow, the children will be provided the opportunity to reinforce their ability to discriminate between properties. There will be various sorting activities which will be based on one or more property.

To start this lesson, each youngster is given a collection of buttons of four different sizes—but of one color. Place the buttons in small boxes. Approximately ten buttons of each size can be placed in each box: a total of about forty buttons per box. Initially encourage the children to discuss the differences and similarities in the collection of buttons each has at his desk. Then suggest sorting the buttons according to some property. After making this suggestion, give the children plenty of time to sort and manipulate the buttons. Paper plates can be passed out to the children. Sorting the buttons on paper plates will be helpful to the children and hopefully reduce the number which find their way to the floor. After the sorting has apparently been completed, encourage individuals to tell the class what property of the buttons they used to make their grouping. It seems obvious that one method of sorting should be to group buttons by size. Most children will probably do it in this manner, but don't rule out other possibilities. There are no right or wrong ways to sort. Some children may not want to sort the buttons, but make some design on the desk top. If so, discuss the design and let the youngster tell you what he is doing. Other children may sort as to side: one pile of green one side up and another pile of green the opposite side up. Is there an up and a down to a button?

At this point, pass out construction paper and see if you can get the children to record their grouping scheme. Some may wish to draw circles for buttons and color these circles with crayons.

61

This will form the beginning of their attempt to record information. Interesting recording schemes may develop in this activity. Possibly some mature groups can be encouraged to write numerals to the right of each picture representing the number of sorted items in each group. Have the children save these papers in an individual folder.

After the recording activity has started, pass out to each youngster two additional buttons, both the same size as one of the sizes in their collection, but a *different* color. Observe what the children do with these "wild buttons." Allow time for children to decide how they wish to deal with these two extra buttons. Some may start a new pile; some will place them in piles already formed; some will make them part of their desk-top design. Inquire as to the reason for each decision.

*Lesson 4*

Lesson 4 is a continuation of Lesson 3. In this lesson, colored tablets are distributed to the children. These tablets are cut from cardboard in various shapes: rectangles, squares, circles, and half circles. Place assortments of different colored tablets in envelopes and distribute one to each child. Approximately thirty to forty tablets per envelope is sufficient. Paper plates may or may not be advisable for this activity. The tablets will slide more easily over the desk top than on the paper plate. Do not discuss with the class the differences and similarities of the objects in the envelope. Suggest sorting the tablets according to some property. This suggestion may not be necessary, for on the basis of the previous lesson it is possible that most or at least some will start this activity immediately. After you have allowed sufficient time for the sorting activity, encourage the children to discuss their sorting technique, requiring that they explain what property or properties they used to determine their arrangements.

Remember, there are a number of ways in which these tablets can be sorted: by shape only, independent of color; by color only, independent of shape; by color and shape, etc. As in Lesson 3 encourage the children to record their results. Pass out construction paper and see what develops. Recording the sorting operation in this lesson will be more difficult than in the previous one because of the many different shapes and colors involved.

After the children have recorded their findings, distribute one diamond-shaped tablet (any color) to each youngster and ask the children to position this tablet in what they consider to be the right spot. Encourage the children to discuss how they decided where this "wild tablet" should fit into their sorting pattern. Some will put it with other shapes the same color; some will place it with the triangle, for it most closely approximates this shape; some will make an entirely separate pile with this one shape, while others will make it part of some design they have formed on their desk tops. The results should be interesting. Remember, the decision each child makes is not as important as his reasons for making the decision.

The shapes used in this lesson all have accepted geometeric names. Using these names in talking about these shapes is desirable. Write the names on the board. It is important that caution be exercised when the names are introduced. Remember, the main purpose of this lesson is *not* the learning of the names for the various shapes. The names can be included as an "added attraction" if carefully done.

Keep developing the "properties word chart"; the list of descriptive words should be increasing daily.

### Lesson 5

In this lesson commonplace objects are used. Each youngster should receive an envelope with a collection of flat washers, lock washers, hexagonal nuts, star washers, and square nuts. Thirty to forty objects in each envelope is sufficient. Ask the youngsters to guess what is in the envelopes before they open them. Point out that visual observation of objects is usually the most effective way of describing them. This comment may be offered by the children.

Once the envelopes are opened, the objects discovered should provoke a general discussion. Describing the properties of these objects can be an interesting class discussion. Emphasize similarities and differences between objects (on paper plates) based on some property of the objects. Allow the

children to comment on what property or properties they used to sort their collection of objects. There are many possibilities—more with this collection possibly than with the other collections.

Pass out construction paper and have the youngsters record their groupings. The combination of a picture and numbers may have become a normal pattern for some children. Certainly, this will not be true for all children, but don't force it.

After the recording has been completed, distribute to each youngster two brass washers and observe how these washers are handled by each child. As before, the child's decision is not as important as his reason for making it.

Because of the similarity between this lesson and previous ones, comments made relative to other lessons apply equally well to this one.

NOTE: Start collecting small jars—baby food jars, peanut butter jars, etc., in preparation for Lesson 8.

## Lesson 6

In this lesson each youngster is given a collection of nuts and bolts. It is hoped by this time the children have reached a certain level of sophistication in dealing with objects. In this lesson many outcomes are possible and it will be challenging to the teacher to explore some of these possibilities.

The collection each child receives should consist of three quarter-inch bolts (3 inches long, full thread) and four quarter-inch nuts. These items can be placed in envelopes and handled in a manner similar to the colored shapes of Lesson 4.

Encourage discussion of the properties of these

nuts and bolts. The word "thread" has different meanings in reference to a bolt or nut, or to sewing. Explore this word. What does the bolt or nut thread do? Can you put the nut on the bolt? How does the nut move on the bolt? Are the threads like stair steps to the nut? Many other questions will come to mind.

A game is now possible. Ask the children to divide the bolt in half using one nut. Correct phrasing of this question is important, but however it is phrased *do not* explain the question by doing the operation yourself in front of the class.

Only a few children may understand at first—and the others may get the idea by watching their neighbors. This is a form of observation, and in this situation it is better than being told what to do by the teacher. Now other questions can follow. Divide the bolt into three parts with two nuts. Can two bolts be joined together? (Yes, using one nut.) When two bolts are joined together, other problems can be suggested. There are obvious advantages to this type of "number work." Use your imagination!

## Lesson 7

In this lesson the properties of leaves will be considered and, as in previous lessons, discussion of these properties (similarities and differences) will be paramount. Then various sorting activities will be conducted in which the children's ability to differentiate and categorize will be tested.

Leaves are an interesting group of objects. Children are interested in leaves and in most cases they are readily available. A few activities with leaves will be briefly described. The teacher can devise many others.

Leaves from a single kind of tree can be collected, their similarities and differences discussed, and be sorted according to size (large, medium, small).

Leaves from three or four different trees can be collected, their similarities and differences discussed, and be sorted according to size (large, medium, small) and according to shape.

After time has been devoted to these two activities, the teacher can point out that different trees have different leaf shapes and that leaves from the same tree differ mainly in size. These observations

**64**

could be the major generalizations made by the class. In the fall color can become another factor in the sorting.

During this activity, each child should be given a hand magnifying lens to examine more closely the properties of the leaves.

Many interesting words can be added to the properties chart. Some that have been used in describing leaves are crispy, bouncy, rough, smooth, crinkly, pointy—and there are many others. By this time the chart should have a large list of descriptive words. Refer to this chart regularly.

### Lesson 8

Considerable time has been devoted to material objects that are solid. There are other objects the teacher can use in order to generate class response about properties and the classification of objects by some physical property.

Work with liquids and powders will present certain problems, but not insurmountable ones. The nature of these "objects" may, in some cases (especially liquids), prevent allowing each youngster to have his own samples. This word of caution should not be interpreted as a reason for not trying to find the means to give each youngster samples to manipulate at his desk. For example, the use of small plastic vials or screw-top glass jars to contain various powder and liquid samples is one way.

Some liquids to examine might be corn syrup (clear), motor oil, honey, molasses, liquid starch, tea, coffee, condensed milk, cooking oil, vinegar, and water.

What property or properties can be used to sort these liquids into groups? Do all the liquids feel the same? Do all the liquids pour the same? (The properties word chart will increase.) Tasting, smelling, and feeling are good ways to determine properties, although tasting should probably be discouraged.

If the class does not suggest it, maybe the teacher can suggest mixing the liquid samples with water. Place some water in several jars and then have children pour the liquids in the water. Use a wooden tongue depressor to stir. Allow the contents to settle and have the class observe the results. Do this with each liquid sample and discuss observations made by the class.

Powdered samples can be handled in a similar manner. Some sample powders to examine are salt, soda, white cornmeal, flour, yellow cornmeal, powdered milk, sugar, and cornstarch. Feeling and smelling activities should be encouraged. Do all feel or smell the same? What property or properties can be used to sort these powders into groups? How do they mix with water? How do the powders mix with some of our liquids? Explore the many possible activities and allow time for exploration to take place.

# CANDLE MAKING

## How to Begin

In this unit children become actively involved in the scientific process of investigation with the use of inexpensive, readily available materials, and a truly interdisciplinary approach to learning can be fostered.

This unit can be coupled with a social studies lesson about early colonial times in America. For example, during a study of the early settlers, chil-

dren may appreciate the fact that the Pilgrims had no electricity nor many of the other comforts that we take for granted.

The candles which the Pilgrims used they made themselves from melted animal fat, called tallow, and beeswax. Many of the Pilgrims did not have the luxury of candle molds and had to hand-dip their candles.

### How to Do It

First fill an iron kettle with candle wax. Then set the kettle in a pan of water on a hot plate. This kettle should be set over a *low heat.* Color red by adding red crayon as the wax melts. It takes some time for the wax to melt. When the wax is just above the melting point it is ready to start dipping candles.

A teacher trying this for the first time should start heating the wax upon arrival in the morning, or well in advance of the time planned for dipping. A double boiler or large fruit juice can be used instead of the iron kettle.

Each child should have his own piece of wicking tied to a small stick. Have the children dip their wicking into the wax, hold it momentarily to drip and straighten it by gently pulling on the wick. The children are eager to watch their candles grow.

The dipping process may be tiring for some of the children and an opportunity for them to sit down and relax should be provided. The children may sing as they walk around the room or listen to records. This allows time for the candles to cool before the next dip. Remind the students to keep their candles vertical so that they will form straight. Youngsters will soon learn that holding the wick in the hot wax longer does not make their candles grow bigger, but only melts off layers that are already formed.

Place poles between two chairs, just as the Pilgrims did, and have the children hang their candles between the poles to harden.

Cardboard candle holders with metal centers may be purchased and decorations of dried cones and seedpods collected by the class can be applied. Glue will hold these in place and a final touch of gold spray or clear lacquer can make an impressive gift for parents at Christmastime.

To provide some contrast the teacher may also use a candle mold to show the children how much faster and more uniform candles may be made in this manner. Many areas of the curriculum can be correlated during this experience. It might be stimulated by social studies and become a science project during the actual candle making. Handwriting and language arts may become involved as the class writes their story of candle making. Drawing pictures to illustrate stories and a field trip to visit a candle-making shop might be included.

At the conclusion of the practical part of candle making the youngsters may be given an opportunity to investigate the properties of a burning candle. After dividing the class into two equal groups, carefully light a candle and place it on an asbestos

mat for each group to examine. Then ask each child to take a good look at the burning candle and make a comment about what he has observed. The results should be rather unusual, judging from the following list of actual observations. Instruct the children that once someone has made an observation, no one else can use it. A great deal can be learned by simply observing a burning candle. The teacher should encourage the children to look carefully at the candle as it continues to burn and not be too concerned with the "correctness" of the pupils' answers. Emphasis should instead be placed upon whether the students' comments are based upon their own perceptions and not what the child is "supposed to see." The question "What is it that is doing the burning?" may result in some surprising answers. Most adults will find that they are hard-pressed to describe what is really happening.

Observations About the Lighted Candle (actual responses made by youngsters in the primary grades).

It's melting.

It looks like water in the center of the candle.

It smells something like oil

It looks like wax.

It's red near the wick.

It's hot!

There's liquid in it.

When you feel it, it feels waxy.

There's a little blue inside the flame.

The inside is getting lower and lower.

It's giving off heat.

It gets smaller as the fire burns it.

It's warm on my hands.

The wax is burning.

If you blow it out, it won't melt anymore.

The teacher blew out the candle, held a match two inches away in the smoke, and the candle lit— "as if by magic," said the children.

The wax is yellow.

Candle is white on the sides.

Around the edges of the candle a little loop is seen.

The wick is now turning black.

The fire is burning the little piece of wick and it's getting black.

Note: It is easy to confuse observations with interpretations. It is an observation to say that the flame gives off heat, or that the candle material becomes a liquid and seems to disappear; it is an interpretation to state the presumed composition of the liquid material (wax).

# CHANGING THINGS

### How to Begin

Chemistry is the study of the composition of matter (ingredients present), the properties of matter (qualities by which materials are recognized), and the changes in composition of matter (transforming one material to another).

Primary children do not have this understanding of chemistry. There is no reason why they should. They do know that their world is made of "things"—objects, materials, or substances.

"Things" put together make new "things." Surely they have observed the results of water mixed with cement, milk added to flour, water added to plaster of paris, the disappearance of a candle as it burns, the dissolving of sugar in tea or coffee, the burning of wood, and the fizz of bubbles in a freshly opened bottle of soda. These are all examples of matter undergoing some kind of change. In this unit the primary youngster will identify or classify some of these combinations and changes in combinations of matter. Simple household materials will be used in all activities.

### Why Do It This Way?

Direct contact with substances undergoing change will provide experiences through which early understandings of the composition of matter can initially develop. Children know that scientists can develop all sorts of new materials. Their immediate environment provides this evidence. This unit will begin to focus attention on some features of chemical combination.

## How to Do It

For convenience this unit is subdivided into lessons. Materials required are listed at the beginning of each lesson. Each lesson does not necessarily represent one class period for science.

### Lesson 1

Materials needed: test tubes (baby food jars can be used), test tube holders (milk cartons—see Thickness of Fluids Unit), hand magnifiers, baking soda, water, paper cups, soda straw scoops, vinegar, and newspapers to cover the desk tops.

Commence the lesson by talking about some substances that are familiar to the children. Discuss the characteristics (color, smell, feel, taste, thickness, etc.) of substances such as milk, honey, flour, gasoline, soda, oil, salt, vinegar, butter, and many others. This discussion can lead to a consideration of how these "things" are made, what they are made of, and ultimately the nature of the process which joins substances together to make new substances.

Suggest the following class activity with baking soda (sodium bicarbonate). Provide each pair of children with a test tube, test tube holder, baking soda (in a small cup), and soda straw scoop. Each pair should place about four soda straw scoops of baking soda in their test tube. Instruct the children to add a little water (to a height of two inches above the bottom of the test tube) and then stir with a straw. Encourage them to use the magnifier as they observe what happens.

The baking soda will not completely dissolve in the water. The children will observe that most of it settles in the bottom of the test tube and some "pieces" float up and down in the water like snowflakes blown by the wind. Observe this with a hand magnifier.

Repeat this experience using a clean dry test tube, only this time have the children add vinegar instead of water. The vinegar is contained in paper cups. Very little vinegar is necessary, for when the vinegar and baking soda unite there is an immedi-

ate reaction. This reaction rapidly produces carbon dioxide, creating many bubbles. The children will want to repeat this experiment. The excitement generated by this experience will not be conducive to talking about it immediately. It is probably wise to reserve discussion for another session. The children will note that the more vinegar they add the more violent is the reaction.

Whenever your class discusses this experience concentrate your questions on what the children observed. The results of this discussion can focus attention on the following points:

(a) Nothing appeared to happen when water and baking soda were mixed.

(b) A rapid reaction occurred when vinegar and baking soda were mixed.

(c) A gas was formed when vinegar was used.

(d) We know it was a gas because bubbles were formed and gases cause bubbles.

(e) A new substance (carbon dioxide gas) was formed when vinegar and baking soda were mixed.

(f) If more vinegar and baking soda were used, more bubbles would be made—that is, more gas.

Try the following demonstration for your class. Place one half teaspoon of baking soda in a balloon and some vinegar in a test tube (two inches from the bottom). Holding the test tube upright, fit the balloon over the end of the test tube. After the balloon is secured, invert the test tube, permitting the vinegar and baking soda to react. The gas formed will inflate the balloon!

Perform this demonstration again, but before mixing the vinegar and baking soda, balance the "balloon-test tube" arrangement on an equal arm balance. After mixing, put it back on the balance and note that there is no change in the setting for the balance. No material has been lost! One experience such as this is not sufficient to proclaim support for the law of conservation of mass but it does represent a beginning. Before placing the balloon-test tube arrangement back on the balance you might question the class about what they think will happen. Some may believe that it will "weigh" less because gases are not heavy; others may think it will "weigh" more because another substance has "been added" by this reaction. This demonstration should create considerable discussion and raise new questions.

*Lesson 2*

Materials needed: test tubes, test tube holders (milk cartons—see Thickness of Fluids Unit), hand magnifiers, lime water, straws, chalk, vinegar, newspapers for the desk tops, and calcium hydroxide.

The children will certainly want to know what kind of gas was liberated in the baking soda-vinegar reaction. Defer giving a direct answer to that question and proceed to the activity in this lesson. This lesson will result in the development of a test for the type gas evolved in the experience of Lesson 1.

The children may have already learned from other sources that they breathe oxygen to live and that they exhale a gas called carbon dioxide. Assuming they possess this knowledge, they can be introduced to a simple test for the presence of carbon dioxide.

Supply each child with a test tube half filled with lime water (calcium hydroxide) and a drinking straw. Instruct the children to place the straw in the test tube and blow into it *gently*. What do they observe? The lime water turns cloudy, indicating the presence of carbon dioxide. The white substance which forms is calcium carbonate (insoluble in water), which eventually will settle to the bottom. During this settling process the liquid appears cloudy. It will be necessary to tell the children that this test is one way to indicate the presence of carbon dioxide.

Now return to the experience in Lesson 1. Is the gas liberated carbon dioxide? Demonstrate this test by bubbling the gas evolved through the lime water as indicated by the diagram.

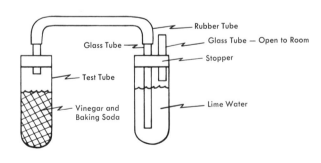

The children can try another reaction in which carbon dioxide is liberated. Supply each child with a one-half-inch piece of chalk to place in a clean test tube. To each test tube add enough vinegar to cover the chalk. Examine the chalk carefully and you will see bubbles of gas (carbon dioxide) forming.

In discussion with your class begin to give consideration to the following broad concepts about the experiences in Lessons 1 and 2:

(a) When a new substance was formed it was always the result of at least two other substances reacting together.

(b) The characteristics of the new substance formed were very different from those of the substances from which it was formed.

(c) Not all substances react together to form new substances.

(d) Tests can be devised for determining the nature of new substances formed.

*Lesson 3*

In the previous experiences a major result of each reaction was the production of carbon dioxide gas. The teacher can now perform some class demonstrations with carbon dioxide which emphasize its use in fire protection.

1. Place a teaspoonful of baking soda in a small jar (one half pint milk jar). Add four teaspoons of vinegar, but do not stir. The bubbling will be the formation of carbon dioxide. Wait until the bubbling stops. Now the upper portion of the jar will contain carbon dioxide. Insert a burning splint, match (long one), or tightly wrapped piece of paper. The carbon dioxide will extinguish the flame.

2. Make some foamite. Children have seen pictures of this in current magazines and on television in cases of emergency plane landings. Burning oil or gasoline cannot be extinguished by water. A special kind of substance which clings and covers burning oil is necessary. Foamite contains bubbles of carbon dioxide in a jelly-like substance. Place two teaspoons of baking soda in a tall drinking glass. Add

two teaspoons of powdered gelatin and two teaspoons of alum. Mix these dry powders thoroughly and then add six teaspoons of vinegar. Stir this mixture rapidly during the formation of the heavy foam. This jelly-like substance, containing carbon dioxide, clings firmly to the glass.

### Lesson 4

Materials needed: baby food jars, filter paper, test tubes, test tube holders, starch, sugar, and newspapers for the desk tops.

"Things" (substances) dissolve in other "things" (substances). Children know that sugar makes things sweet when it is mixed with other things. They have seen some of the undissolved sugar in the bottom of iced tea glasses. During a class discussion the children can provide many examples of two or more "things" (substances) which have been mixed together. Some examples are chocolate milk, ice cream soda, vegetable soup, and salad dressing.

These mixtures can be separated by filtration. The children can try to filter a mixture. They should work together in pairs. Provide each pair with two baby food jars and two pieces of filter paper. Have the children prepare in separate test tubes a mixture of sugar and water (half a teaspoon of granulated sugar) and a mixture of starch (cornstarch) and water (half a teaspoon of cornstarch). Show the children how to fold the filter paper and insert it into the jar. Now have them pour the sugar-water solution and the starch-

water solution into separate filter papers. They will observe that the sugar is not filtered out (taste the water which comes through) but the starch is filtered out (the water which comes through is clear). The starch will be in the filter paper.

This experience can lead to a discussion of methods used to separate substances (filtering is one). Some materials will not pass through a filter and this is the basis for filtration methods of purifying water. The discussion should point out that all substances cannot be separated by filtering and that this is only one of the many techniques the scientist uses in examining various substances.

This unit introduces primary children to some of the ways substances combine and how they can be separated. Discussions should shape more questions than answers. There can be additional student-centered activities or teacher demonstrations. Some are suggested in the list below.

1. Mixtures: all substances do not unite. Children can experiment with mixtures. Try the following:

   (a) A jar containing five marbles and three or four teaspoonfuls of sugar. Add water and stir. Do the marbles unite with the sugar? Can the marbles be removed without removing the sugar? Does anything happen to the sugar-water solution when the marbles are removed?

   (b) A jar containing iron filings and sugar—about equal amounts of each. Add water and stir. Do the iron filings unite with the sugar? Can the iron filings be removed? How? What happens to the sugar when the iron filings are removed?

   (c) Salt and sugar, equal parts, mixed in water would be a more difficult problem for the children. Consider the problem of separating this mixture while still in the dry form. Consider the same problem after it has been mixed with water.

2. Compounds: the result of substances which do chemically unite. Children have already experienced this in earlier activities of this unit. Try the following as class demonstrations:

(a) Burn a lump of sugar. Construct a small aluminum foil holder (spoon-shaped) to contain the sugar. The source of heat can be an alcohol burner.

(b) Mix some lemon juice from a lemon with a small amount of baking soda.

(c) Obtain a few pieces of liver from the local butcher. Cut the liver into *very small pieces* (preferably mashed up) and place in a convenient container. Add some hydrogen peroxide and note the chemical reaction. This demonstration can be used not only to show a chemical reaction but as a means to reveal how the human stomach "attacks" food particles.

It is important to keep in focus your major objectives: student recognition that substances combine to form new substances; that there are tests for identifying characteristics of substances; that certain procedures will result in separating substances; and the maximum involvement of the children in making decisions.

# EARTHWORMS

### How to Begin

This unit is designed for use either in the fall or in the spring. Choose a time when earthworms may be found outdoors. It may be used over a period of about four weeks, two times each week, depending on the sustained interest and enthusiasm of the children. The teacher might stimulate interest in these animals by maintaining an earthworm farm in the classroom. Directions for making such a farm are provided in Lesson 1.

Encourage the children to find worms at home. Each child could be responsible for bringing in his own earthworm for study. Give the children ample time to observe, experiment, and record. Observations should be recorded either as a group, or individually by children who are able to devise a simple method of recording what they find.

Do not be limited by the lessons given here. They are merely suggestions. Your children will ask questions and together you may think of new ways of finding the answers. The exploratory behavior of earthworms to be examined should be selected as much as possible by the children.

In this unit, the children, through studying about one small animal, will learn not only about the earthworm, but also more about their environment and themselves.

All living things need a suitable environment and many have made adaptations to live in that environment. An adequate supply of food, water, and air is necessary. Earthworms, like all other living things, take in material from their surroundings and use these materials to keep themselves alive. Our observations and learnings will help us to understand how they do this.

An earthworm hatches from a cocoon and resembles an adult earthworm. It matures and reproduces its own kind. Reproduction is necessary for life to continue. The reproductive system of the earthworm is well developed. It consists of male and female parts which are located in the same worm. One worm, however, cannot be both mother and father of its own offspring!

73

Earthworms respond to stimuli, or changes in their environment. Light, heat, cold, sound, and pressure are some of the stimuli to which they respond. How and why they respond are some of the things we will observe. Many of these responses are instinctive. Are the responses learned? Can an earthworm learn? Perhaps we can try an experiment to see if an earthworm learns.

## Why Do It This Way?

Children are *familiar* with this common animal which is found wherever there is moist soil. Young anglers have used them as bait on their fishing expeditions. Young farmers have encountered them while digging in the soil in their own back yards. Almost everyone has seen them on top of the ground after a heavy rain.

Earthworms are *plentiful* enough so that each child can have his own specimen for study. The teacher can maintain a larger terrarium for further study.

Earthworms are interesting both in physical characteristics and habits. Children should be encouraged to make comparison of themselves and earthworms. The earthworm, like the human, has many parts and systems but they are much simpler.

Thus, a study of the earthworm helps us to understand not only one important life form, but also provides us with information basic to the study of all higher forms of animal life.

Many interesting words can be added to the children's vocabulary during the study of the earthworm. Descriptive words, name words, and other unusual words can be used in charts, records, stories, and displays. Write the words on the chalkboard and on labels for the children to see as they are using them. A few are suggested here.

| | |
|---|---|
| earthworm | posterior |
| tunnel | segments |
| burrow | hibernation |
| castings | stimulus |
| setae | bristles |
| anterior | humus |

*Earthworm Unit*

Materials needed: one per student

  Worms
  Small containers
  Soil
  One large bowl or terrarium
  Paper towels
  Newspaper
  Magnifying lens
  Oatmeal and/or other cereals
  Flashlights

Optional: one per every two students (supplied by students)

  Thermometers
  Dry cell wires
  Sandpaper

This unit has been divided into lessons, mainly for convenience. Each lesson does not necessarily represent one day's work but instead should take as long as is needed if interest is high.

### Lesson 1   Making a Worm Farm

The following procedure can be used to maintain earthworms in the classroom.

*Container:* Any large, wide-mouthed glass jar, tank, terrarium, or fishbowl may be used.

*Soil:* Some gravel may cover the bottom. Add loosely packed, slightly moist soil containing much humus (decaying plant and animal material).

*Worms:* Children may collect worms at home or teacher and children may go as a group to the schoolyard and dig for worms. Dig down about twelve inches into the soil. Lift soil out carefully and sift through it. Usually worms are in garden soil. If there are no worms, probably the soil is too dry, hard-packed, and/or lacking in decaying plant and animal material that worms need for food. Worms may be also purchased commercially from biological supply houses.

*Care:* Add worms to your prepared container. Worms eat many different kinds of food. Feed the worms with bits of lettuce, cornmeal, oatmeal, and other cereals mixed into the top layers of soil.

Keep the worm farm cool, slightly damp, but never wet, and always have some worm food in the soil. Plants may be grown in the container also.

### Lesson 2   First Observations

Materials: paper towels, earthworms.

Each child should have his earthworm in its own container. Ask them to take their worms out carefully and place them on pieces of moist paper towel.

Let them observe the worms carefully. Each may pick up his worm and compare it with a classmate's worm.

The classroom discussion should take its course freely and the children can make remarks about their observations, describing what they see and feel.

The teacher should write down the children's observations or give them time to record as best they can. Accept all comments without approval or disapproval.

Make a separate list of the questions children ask.

Do not try to accomplish too much during the first lesson. Allow the students an opportunity to reflect upon their observations.

Return worms carefully to their respective containers.

Begin a vocabulary list of words used during the unit.

### Lesson 3   How Does an Earthworm Move?

Materials: earthworms ready for study, mirrors, pieces of glass, magnifying glasses.

Teacher may lead the class discussion about movement or locomotion, using the following questions:

How do you move from place to place?

What parts of your body do you use?

What parts of your body do you use when you eat?

Does your earthworm have arms? Legs?

How do you tell the front (anterior) from the back (posterior)?

How does the earthworm move on your desk?

How does a baby first learn to move?

Have some child demonstrate how a baby crawls. How is the earthworm's crawling different from yours? (The earthworm instead of the front part pulling all the rest of its body each time, several parts of its body are holding on and pulling up the parts behind them. One way to observe the earthworm is to put it on a mirror. Another way is to put it on a piece of glass and watch it from underneath. A magnifying glass will help the children observe more carefully. Children may observe that some parts become thinner and longer.)

Use a slinky toy to help illustrate how earthworms move.

What helps the earthworm grip the ground?

Hold your earthworm in your hand. Can you feel anything? (Because this is hard to see teacher should explain: Earthworms have structures which help them grip the ground. They are tiny, hard bristles in the skin which are called setae. They are found on all segments except those near the ends. Use magnifying glasses to see better.)

*Lesson 4* How Does an Earthworm Move Through Soil?

Ask the question "How does the earthworm move through the soil?" and let the children describe the possible ways in which earthworms accomplish this.

(It literally eats its way through. The animal takes in dirt and other material, digests the food available, and excretes the remaining soil. In this way earthworms help cultivate the soil. Their burrowing keeps the ground soft and loose so that rain can soak down to the roots of plants.)

"Now let's perform an experiment to see how the earthworms burrow." (If the teacher has main-tained a worm farm in the classroom, the children may be able to see the burrows along the side of the glass. If not, try the following teacher demonstration.)

"The movement of an earthworm through soil can be studied in the classroom. You will need two pieces of glass [five inches square is large enough], masking tape, some strips of cardboard, soil, and a worm. Separate the edges of the two sheets of glass on three sides with narrow strips of cardboard, and fasten these edges with masking tape. The sheets of glass should be about a half inch apart. Fill the space between the glass with soil. Moisten the soil slightly with water. Stand the glass plates on edge, the open part on top. Place the worm on top of the soil. It can be observed through the glass as it burrows through the soil." (To last longer, wood may be used instead of cardboard.)

*Lesson 5* Experiments with Earthworms and Light

Do earthworms usually go toward light or away from it?

1. Have the children place their earthworms on a desk. Have a light source coming from one direction. Do the earthworms usually go toward or away from the light source? Does the light seem to make any difference? Record the observations of all the children at several different times of the day and on different days if possible.
2. Set up a box divided with one side covered and dark, the other side open so light can shine in (or use a flashlight). Try several worms. What happens? (Keep a record of what happens.) Does the worm seem to prefer one side of the box to the other side?
3. Place a plastic tube in a box. Place an earthworm in the tube. Does it move towards the other end, or does it stay in one spot? Put the top on the box. Will the earthworm react differently? What happens? How many times should you run tests like this? Can you draw any conclusions?

Questions for discussion:

Does an earthworm have eyes?

What might take the place of eyes for an earthworm?

Where do the worms usually live?

Does it need light?

When does it usually come out of the earth?

Is it light when it comes out?

4. Experiment to see the difference between light and dark for yourself without using your eyes. Use a lamp and a piece of dark cloth for a blindfold. Have more than one switch or clicking sound. When a child has been blindfolded turn the light on and off to see if he is aware of its being lighter or darker without having his eyes open. This may be done in a darkened room with the whole class *if* the children will all close their eyes. Can an earthworm detect light even without eyes?

### Lesson 6    Experiment with Cold

How do earthworms react to cold things?

1. Place an ice cube near your worm. What does he do? Does he touch it? Does he move away? How does your earthworm react?

2. Use a box or box cover. In one side put cold dirt (kept in refrigerator overnight); in the other side put soil at room temperature. Place earthworm in center. What happens? Where does he go? Try another combination: soil that has stood in the sun and very wet soil; cold moist soil and hot moist soil.

3. Place a piece of metal near an earthworm. Observe.

Question: What does the earthworm do in the winter, when it is very cold?

For discussion: How does an earthworm keep warm? Does it keep warm in the same way that people do?

### Lesson 7    Experiment with Colors

Do earthworms prefer one color to another?

On one piece of paper paste four equal-size pieces of yellow, brown, red, and black paper (or use other combinations of color). In the center make a white circle.

Place the earthworm in the center.

Does it go to one color more than another?

How many times should you have a worm try?

How many worms should be used?

Keep a record of how many times a certain worm left the paper by one color. Did it cross two colors? Did it stay on one? What else happened? Did it seem to search around for a special place? Was that because it was headed in that direction?

Do you think earthworms like one color better than the others. If your answer is "Yes," why? Do you think earthworms can tell one color from another? Do you believe that they can "see" color the way we do? What other experiments with color might you try with earthworms?

### Lesson 8    Shoebox Ecology

Divide a shoe box into three equal parts and place different kinds of soil (humus, sand, and gravel) in each section. Next divide the sand into two equal lengthwise portions. Dampen one part with water and leave the other part dry.

| Wet humus | Wet sand | Wet gravel |
|-----------|----------|------------|
| Dry humus | Dry sand | Dry gravel |

Place three earthworms, one in each of the different dry sections of the box. Have the children keep a record of the length of time the earthworms move about and in which section they finally come to rest.

This may be simplified by taking a box and putting sand in one end and moist soil in the other and observing the results.

### Lesson 9   How Worms Stay Alive: Food

Materials: different soil samples, newspapers, model of an earthworm, or a large drawing.

Questions for discussion: Why do earthworms need food? Where do they get their food? Do people need food? Do we get food in similiar ways to earthworms?

(Earthworms get food mostly from plant materials—leaves, seeds, or other parts. Soil contains small bits of dead animal and plant material which are food to an earthworm.)

Examine soil samples. What can you see? Are there any bits of dead animal and plant material in sandy soil? In humus?

Teacher may show parts of digestive system on model or drawing and explain that the earthworm takes food into its body through its mouth. Who can find the earthworm's mouth on the model? Does it have jaws or teeth? (Food is broken down to very small particles by grinding it and treating it with special chemicals—enzymes. This is called digestion. Digestions occurs in the alimentary canal. This is the thin inner tube which runs the length of the body. Food is taken in through the opening at the front end, the mouth. It is then moved along by the action of the muscles. Whatever is not used leaves the body by the opening at the rear end, the anus. The material which leaves the body is called castings. Castings help keep soil fertile).

Do earthworms digest their food in the same way we do? (The alimentary canal of the earthworm and the human are quite similar, even some of the names are the same. The blood vessels then distribute food to all the cells.)

### Lesson 10   How Worms Stay Alive: Air

Materials: containers of soil, pitchers of water.

All living things need air. Animals living underground need air. (Oxygen is in air.) Earthworms live underground. Is there oxygen in soil?

Experiment to find out: Place some soil in a container (glass or clear plastic). Add water to cover soil. What happens? (This can be done in small groups. Children can watch the bubbles rise.) What does this show us?

How do we get air into our bodies? Take a deep breath. We breathe through our noses to get air into and out of our lungs. (How do you think the earthworm gets air? The earthworm uses its moist skin to get oxygen into its body. What would happen if the earthworm's skin dried out? If the skin becomes dry, oxygen can't move through it.)

What happens to the soil during a heavy rain? Have you ever seen earthworms on the sidewalk or road after a heavy rain? What caused them to go there? Sometimes they die. What do you think killed them?

## Questions to Think About

1. How does the earthworm travel on top of the ground? Underground?
2. Can the earthworm go backwards? When might he go backwards?
3. Can you tell which end is the head (anterior)? Which is the back (posterior) of the earthworm?
4. Notice the bristles. What do they help the earthworm to do?
5. See the rings around the earthworm. They are called_____. Can you count them?
6. Can you find the thick place? It is called the _____.
7. Why does the earthworm feel moist when you touch it?
8. What color is the earthworm?
9. Are all earthworms the same size?
10. Can you see the earthworm's eyes? Do you think he can see where he is going? How? Can he tell the difference between light and dark?
11. Where does the earthworm usually live?
12. Why do you suppose an earthworm comes up out of the ground during a storm?
13. Why do earthworms die on top of the ground?
14. How is the earthworm useful to farmers?
15. How is the earthworm useful to fishermen? To birds? To some other animals? To plants?
16. What might kill an earthworm?
17. What does an earthworm do in winter?
18. During a long dry spell why might you not be able to find any earthworms in the soil?
19. How are earthworms born? Do they lay eggs? Do they have babies like humans?

*Lesson 11*  Comparison of the Behavior of the Earthworm with Other Kinds of Animals

I. Compare earthworms and pet hamsters.
   A. How are they alike? When are they most active?
   Both are nocturnal (night) animals.
   Both are naturally burrowing animals.
   Both need food, water, and air, but they get them in different ways.
   Both eat plants or parts of plants.

   B. How are they different?
   They live in different places.
   Hamsters have eyes, ears, and feet. Earthworms do not have any of these things.
   Mother hamsters give birth to live babies. Earthworms each have a cocoon which passes into the soil where young earthworms hatch.
   Back cover of the earthworm.
   Body covering is different. The way they move is different. Compare.
   How do you feed a pet hamster? How do you feed earthworms, if you keep them in a container?

II. Compare goldfish. Use same type of questions as above.

III. Compare with cats; dogs; other pets that children are familiar with.

IV. Compare an earthworm with yourself. (Allow children to formulate the questions.)

# EMBRYOS

### How to Begin

The egg is the beginning structure for all life. An experience-oriented approach to this beginning of life will help children to understand that animals, including humans, produce eggs.

From an awareness of new life in the early spring the teacher may lead the class to a discussion of eggs. All living things that lay eggs come from eggs. There are many different kinds of eggs. This unit can begin with a discussion of what the children's concepts of an egg are.

### How to Do It

*Lesson 1*

Some general questions and observations of a hen's egg.

Have the children bring eggs from home or, better still, arrange to purchase them from the school cafeteria. Instruct the children each to pick up a hen's egg. Ask them to hold it in their hands and examine it carefully. How strong is the shell? Squeeze the egg gently but firmly. Does it feel strong? How thick do you think the shell is? Can anyone think of a way in which we might be able to measure the thickness? Are the shells of all eggs the same thickness? Compare your egg with others in the room. Is the shell solid or does it have little holes? Hold it up to the light. Can you see little holes? (Questions concerning the porosity of the shell might have more direct meaning when the eggs are incubated in a later lesson and water must be sprinkled occasionally.) Try to roll the egg. Does the shape have anything to do with the way the egg rolls on a flat surface? Could this shape in any way aid in the protection of the egg?

What color is your egg? Are there any other differences in eggs that are brown?

Encourage free discussion about the outside characteristics of eggs. Children may bring in other eggs or pictures of other eggs. In what ways are

all eggs similar? In what ways are they different?

The discussion can easily move to thoughts about the origin of eggs. Where do they come from? Do animals lay eggs? Do all animals lay eggs? Some animals come from eggs; do people come from eggs? Answers to many of the possible questions are not always necessary—more important is the creation of an atmosphere in which children freely talk about these topics.

### Lesson 2

How about the inside of a hen's egg? What do you think we would find if we broke one open?

Break one or two eggs for the children and pour the contents into a dish or paper plate. A brave teacher will permit each child to open his own egg. Have the desks covered with newspapers and be prepared with a supply of paper towels. Each child should have a pie plate in which to open the eggs and a tongue depressor as a tool to "push the egg around." Listen to the comments as children open their eggs. Some very descriptive words will be used, possibly leading to the construction of a "word chart for eggs."

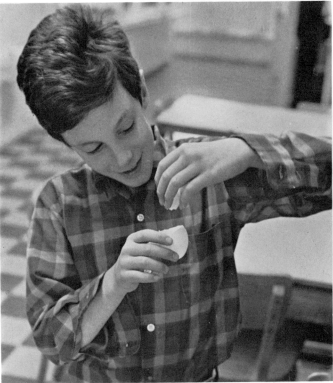

The eggshells should be saved, for there is much to observe about their structure. There are many things for the children to see, and time and patience will be required.

Try to peel the outer shell from an egg and let the class examine it. Observe the flattened end of the egg. Note the air space in this end.

There is white sticky stuff around the center of the egg (protoplasm). The orange-yellow part in the center is called the yolk (nucleus). You may see something coming out of the ends of the center (yolk). (The two twisted strands connecting the inside of the egg to the shell are called the chalaza and are twisted by their spiral path as they come spinning down the oviduct of the hen.)

### Lesson 3

This lesson gives some background information for the teacher and includes suggested questions for classroom discussion. Encourage individual re-

sponses. The teacher should be concerned with finding out what children already know about eggs.

Chicken Eggs: What is a chicken egg? Can we name the parts now? The yolk is the yellow ball in the middle. The watery part surrounding the yolk is the white. It becomes very white when you fry or boil an egg. The yolk tastes good. It is very good food for you and for the baby chick. The baby chick grows inside the yolk. The shell is round and round shapes are very strong. Eggs are round and they will not break open easily. If an egg were square like a box, it would break easily.

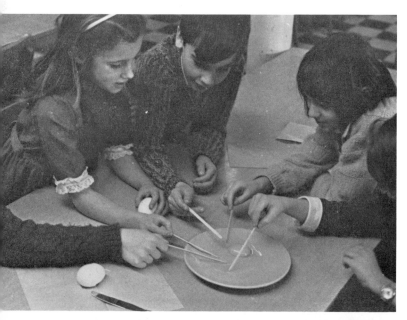

A hen can sit on her eggs and they will not break. An egg standing on end is a very strong structure. At first the chick in the egg is so small you cannot see it. It is like a seed in the center of the yolk. The seed, if fertilized, will grow. After a while the soft mass becomes a baby chick. It will have hard bones, sharp toenails, and a strong beak. A chick will grow inside of an egg when it is kept warm for twenty-one days. The mother hen sits on the egg to keep it warm. The seed in the egg develops into a chick.

How does the baby chick get out? It taps on the shell with its beak. It taps a long time. It makes a little hole in the shell. The shell cracks all the way around. The chick rests a while, then tries again. The chick pushes with its legs too. Then it tumbles out. It is very tired and all wet. The mother hen is dry and warm. Under the mother hen the little chick dries out.

All eggs help to keep the young safe. When the egg hatches, the baby is ready to try and live in the outside world. Other kinds of eggs hatch and grow into fish, frogs, snakes, birds, or platypuses.

*Lesson 4*

Materials needed:

| eggs | cotton | water |
|---|---|---|
| incubator | mash | desk lamp |
| aluminum pie plate | hot plate | fertile eggs |
| | | shoe box |

Before beginning this activity be certain to make arrangements for those chicks that will hatch. Parents' permission for students to take a chick home should be obtained before any eggs are incubated.

Discuss with the children the possibility that some eggs might not hatch and that those that do will have to be properly cared for. In this way the teacher will not be faced with the dilemma of what to do with the chicks after they are hatched. Also, if the children are alerted to the possibility that some of their eggs may not develop, a traumatic situation can be averted.

At the completion of a discussion of different kinds of eggs, and the first lesson on the properties of eggs, the children should enjoy the experience involving the hatching of chicken eggs. Preferably this should be done in the early spring.

Steps to follow:

1. Obtain as many fertilized eggs as can be incubated at one time.
2. Mark X on one side of each egg.
3. Place the eggs in an incubator with the X side up.
4. At the end of six hours turn the eggs so that the X side is down (not absolutely necessary but it helps).
5. Continue to reverse eggs every six hours (or before leaving school and immediately upon arriving in the morning and again at noon).
6. Sprinkle water on eggs twice a day.
7. Be sure the water well in the incubator is full.
8. Temperature of incubator must be maintained between 102 and 104 degrees F.
9. Hatching normally occurs on the twenty-first day.
10. Do not help the chick to get out of the egg. If it can't get out by itself, it probably will not survive.
11. Chick may be removed from incubator after one hour, but should immediately be placed in a brooder.
12. An inexpensive brooder consists of a shoe box under a desk lamp. The chick should be kept warm, but not hot. If you can hold your hand comfortably in the shoe box, temperature is correct.
13. Feed the chicks starter mash.
14. *Do not handle chicks needlessly.*
Note: Eggs need to be turned only between the second and the eighth day, but it is beneficial to turn them throughout incubation.

### Lesson 5

Some information about other animals that lay eggs can serve as an interesting series of discussion periods a few days per week while the children are waiting for the chicken eggs to hatch.

Fish eggs: Fish lay eggs, which stay in the water. They do not have hard shells to protect them. They are usually laid in jelly. The jelly is a kind of glue that permits the eggs to stick together on debris or stones. The eggs do not float away. The

jelly is soft enough for the young to get out when they hatch. Fish eggs will usually stay at the bottom of the water, protected from the waves and wind. The water keeps the eggs warm enough to promote development. The mother fish often watches over the eggs. Eventually the eggs hatch and the baby fish swim away.

Frog eggs: Frogs can live on land and in water, but they lay their eggs in the water. They are tiny and black and are held inside a blob of white jelly. The white jelly part floats with the eggs inside. The jelly is too large for most hungry fish to swallow, and it has an unpleasant taste. The frog eggs are fairly safe inside. When the eggs are ready to hatch, the jelly breaks apart. The young frogs are called tadpoles. Tadpoles live in the water until they grow into mature frogs and then venture forth on land.

Dinosaur eggs: When dinosaurs were alive they laid their eggs on land. The egg was protected by a shell. The egg had a yolk like the chicken egg to feed the baby dinosaur. The dinosaur came out of his shell with reasonably strong arms and legs. Full-grown, a dinosaur was as large as an average-size house. They were larger than elephants. No one has seen a live dinosaur, but their bones and eggs have been found. A dinosaur egg is very big and you would need both hands to carry one.

Snake eggs: Some snakes lay eggs. The shell of a snake egg is soft. But it is very strong too. It is like the soft part of your shoe. Snake eggs are like rubber. A snake egg will bounce if you drop it. Snakes can swim but the egg will sink in water, so the snake lays her eggs on land. The eggs have a yolk and a white but they are not pleasant to eat. When the baby snake hatches, it is ready to live by itself. The mother and father do not feed it.

Platypus eggs: The platypus is the only animal with fur that lays eggs. The platypus lays her eggs in a burrow by a stream. The doorway is under water. No hungry land animals can swim into the doorway. The eggs are safe in the burrow.

Bird eggs: Birds lay eggs. The biggest bird egg is the ostrich egg. It is about as big as a man's fist. The smallest egg is the hummingbird egg. It is about as big as the fingernail on your thumb. There are many kinds of bird eggs. Some eggs are laid in tree trunks and in chimneys. These eggs usually are white and aid the mother in seeing them at night. Some eggs are laid on the ground. They may be striped or dotted all over. They appear to blend in with the ground as a sort of camouflage. Hungry animals do not see them; they are safely hidden. The robin lays blue eggs in her nest. The blue color helps the robin to know that they are her own eggs. The cowbird does not make a nest. She lays her eggs in other birds' nests. Cowbird eggs have specks on them, and if the cowbird lays her speckled eggs in a robin's nest the robin will push them out. The mother robin prefers only her own blue eggs in her nest. Gulls lay their eggs near the seashore. Some birds lay their eggs in nests on rocky cliffs. These eggs are pointed. They roll in a circle, like a funnel or the top of an ice cream cone. The shape keeps the egg from rolling out of the nest or falling off the cliff and breaking.

# FUN WITH A MAGNIFYING GLASS

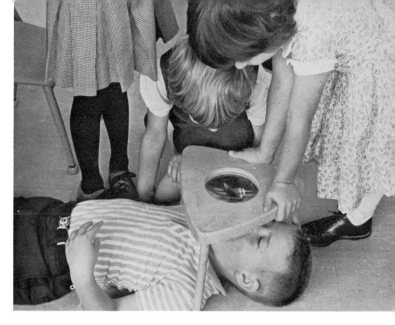

It is not necessary that all units extend for several weeks. A few simple materials in large enough quantity will permit many student-centered activities. One such activity might be labeled "Fun with a Magnifying Glass."

## How to Begin

Obtain one hand magnifier (3 to 5 power) for each child. Collect a wide assortment of objects.

## Why Do It This Way?

The magnifier does something to the way objects appear. Direct contact with this effect through autonomous activities will result in the accumulation of raw experience from which future decisions may result.

## How to Do It

Develop a listing of objects to be viewed. Each child should have this list at his desk. For example, ask: "What do you see when you look at—?"

(1) leaf
(2) coin
(3) print on a newspaper
(4) salt
(5) wood
(6) hair
(7) skin
(8) drop of water
(9) bubbles on the side of a glass of water
(10) insect
(11) drop of oil on water
(12) meat
(13) pond water
(14) tip of a pencil
(15) cotton cloth
(16) nylon stocking

Encourage children to draw pictures of what they see and to describe verbally their observations. Are all observations the same? How do they differ? In what ways are they alike?

Extend some of the observations by presenting specific questions relative to some of the observations. For example, explore the viewing of newsprint with the magnifying glass by using the following questions:

1. Use the magnifying glass to look at a newspaper picture. Draw what you see.
2. Look at a dark spot in the picture. Look at a light spot in the picture. Are they different? Draw what you see each time.
3. Place a ruler on the picture. Use the magnifying glass to count the number of dots in a half inch. How many dots are in an inch?
4. Can you figure out a way to measure distance by counting the dots in a picture?

Unique schemes for measuring can be developed using a magnifier and the dots in a newspaper photograph. Children should be encouraged to invent their own units of standard length.

The magnifying glass can be an exciting tool in the hands of the primary youngster. Direct his activities in its use with imagination and patience.

# GUPPIES

There are probably several million distinct forms of animal life. The largest of these is about ten million times larger than the smallest. Systems have been developed to organize the tremendous diversity found in the animals of our world. At the primary level, some attempt should be made to classify animals as to habit, body forms, and body functions.

Where do animals live? They live in many different places—in caves, in water, in houses, in desert areas, on high mountains, in the air, in forests. What do animals eat? They eat an assortment of various plants and other animals. Do all animals look alike? Not all animals have legs, fins, antennae, shells, eyes, ears, claws, arms, beaks, sharp teeth, fur, wings, noses, etc. Why are all animals not alike? Is it because of where they live—their environment? Are all animals natural enemies of one another? What means of protection do different animals have against the perils of their environment and other animals? Many other questions can be considered. They all serve to point out differences and similarities in the animal kingdom and hence permit classification of these animals according to their similarities and differences.

One effective way to observe and study living systems is through the use of aquaria in the classroom. Commercially produced aquaria are not required. Students can supply their own and as a result have many living communities to observe. Any wide-mouth quart, half-gallon or gallon jar can serve as a suitable container (mayonnaise, peanut butter jars, etc.).

## How to Begin

Obtain six to ten large jars. (White sand in the bottom of each jar is optional.) Fill each jar with fresh water. Let the jars sit for several days before adding living material. Guppies, snails, and pond plants are a good beginning. Magnifying glasses should be available.

## Why Do It This Way?

A major objective in this unit is to direct attention to the similarities and differences in living things. This should include comparisons with people—how people mature and develop and what their basic needs are. Children can make comparisons between their needs and those of the living things they now are more closely observing. In this case, how does a guppy mature, and in what ways are its needs and development similar to those of a human? What is the life cycle of a guppy? Does it resemble that of a human?

Living things are always exciting to young people. This does not mean they are always careful in the manner in which they care for living things. Therefore, a major objective of this unit is to develop an appreciation for humane care of animals. Furthermore, the young child's natural inquisitiveness about living things can be used as a springboard to motivate him to develop some thoughts about living, growing, and dying.

## How to Do It

Start eight or ten aquaria. Probably the best arrangement is two or three children to each aquarium.

For convenience only, the activities in this unit have been subdivided into lessons. One lesson may continue for several class meetings, or, possibly, never stop—always being an intimate part of all other lessons.

*Lesson 1*

Place a pair of guppies (male and female), one snail and some pond plants in each aquarium. The water temperature should be room temperature or warmer (70° to 80°F). These items may be obtained by the children or from a commercial tropical fish dealer. Permit time for the youngsters to observe their own aquarium. Listen to their comments, possibly recording some of them, but do not interrupt or try to interpret their observations. Be a good listener!

It will be necessary for each group of youngsters to locate a safe place for their aquarium. Within reason permit the children to position their aquaria in what they consider to be the best possible locations. The only instruction you provide, once a location is agreed upon, is that the aquarium will remain in this location for most of the unit. The "best location" will differ among groups, which undoubtedly will result in interesting comparisons later in the unit.

## Lesson 2

Probably during the first week there will be little change, allowing the children sufficient time to observe all the aquaria.

The guppy is a small brightly colored fish native to Venezuela and Trinidad. The male guppy has more brilliant coloring than the female. It pays particular attention to the female by "dancing" around it constantly. The male guppy grows to about three-quarters of an inch in length. The female guppy is slow-moving and has a grayish-green color. It produces young that are able to swim and feed at birth. Eggs in the female are fertilized by the male. The male has a specially formed fin in which the fertilizing material is carried. The female produces about fifty young guppies every four to six weeks. Guppies will eat their young.

Children will identify their own guppies in their aquaria. Some may give their guppies names. There will be many comments about "the way they swim," "where they seem to stay most of the time," "they don't seem to like the snails," "the snails are so slow," "will there be baby guppies?" "how long will they live?" "mine can hear when I tap the side of the jar," "they seem to know me," "one is friendlier than the other," "will they die?" "what food do they like?" "do they ever rest?" Statements such as these and many more will freely be offered. Note that many of the comments are the same statements and questions children have about people and the way they live.

## Lesson 3

After a couple of weeks new observations will be made. Some baby guppies may be born, some may die, some will be eaten, the pond snails will have produced jelly-like clusters of eggs on the glass walls, and some changes may be apparent in the water coloration. Water in the jars near the window will begin to turn green while the water in jars in other parts of the room remains clear. As some of the jars turn greener and greener children will express concern and curiosity over this phenomenon.

With several weeks of "raw experience" collected, children are more than prepared to discuss the cycle of life, birth, growth, and death. Do not limit this discussion to guppies and snails but expand it to include people. People are born ready for living; they grow and develop into different sizes and possess different abilities; and eventually people die.

Comparisons between guppies and people should be made. Do guppies live as long as people? Do guppies "get babies" like people do? Do guppies get sick like people do? What do guppies breathe? What do people breathe? Can guppies hear, speak, and smell? Do guppies get hungry? Do people get hungry? Will all baby guppies grow to be strong and healthy? Will all children grow to be strong and healthy? Do guppies love their mother and father? The questions and possible comparisons are innumerable. A patient, understanding teacher will encourage an exciting exchange of thoughts.

*Lesson 4*

Children will continue to express concern about the green water in some of the jars. Many causes will be suggested. Some are convinced that the green plants in the water are responsible and hence will suggest placing a clear jar of water near the window. It will be demonstrated that the plants were not responsible but rather that the sun was in some way causing the green. This will present a dilemma to the children.

The teacher must now supply an assist. Obtain some Volvox, a green algae, from a biological supply house. Volvox is one of some 20,000 kinds of protozoa. It has hairlike projections from its body (called flagella), possesses chlorophyll (providing the green color), moves about in fresh water in a ball of cells and multiplies rapidly. Volvox can be distinguished with the unaided eye, but a hand magnifier is sometimes helpful.

Place a jar containing a culture of Volvox next to a second jar containing a sample of green aquarium water (you may find it advisable to have several such pairs in the class). Supply the children with magnifying glasses and ask them to observe both jars. Tell the children that one jar contains Volvox, which are called algae, and that there are many other kinds of algae. Listen for their descriptions as they use the hand magnifier. Hopefully, the children will relate the green Volvox to the cause for the green coloration in their aquaria. A question to be prepared for is "Where did the green algae come from in my aquarium?" It was already there! The sun helped it to grow.

*Lesson 5*

How do we clean up the water? The children want to know how to "get rid of the algae." This can be accomplished by introducing the water flea—Daphnia—obtainable from a biological supply house. The water flea is a tiny freshwater shellfish (1/10 inch long). It skips and jumps through the water using feelers (antennae) as oars. The body of the water flea is transparent. In the summer months millions of these creatures can be found in ponds and marshes.

The children will be excited by the fast, skipping movement of the water flea. Place the water fleas in the green aquarium water (guppies should not be present). In a matter of a few days the Daphnia will filter out the algae, for they can live completely on algae. The water will again be clear, and it will be noted that the Daphnia population has increased.

*Lesson 6*

How did the Daphnia clear up the water? The children will be interested in this problem and will probably volunteer the thought that the Daphnia ate the algae—which is quite correct!

The water flea is large enough to see with the unaided eye. A hand magnifier (10 power) will permit viewing the transparent water flea more carefully. View the Daphnia through the magnifier after they have been in the "algae water" for a day. The intestines of the water flea will be clearly visible and show it to be stuffed with green algae. The algae were eaten by the water fleas!

What can be concluded from these observations? The water flea must have a mouth—like people. The water flea must have an intestine—like people. The water flea must discard waste material (feces)—like people.

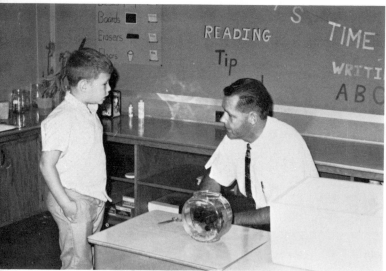

## Lesson 7

After all the aquaria have been cleared up by the Daphnia feed them to the guppies. They will be chased by the guppies and completely consumed. This results in discovering a basic concept: the food chain. Algae appear in the water due to the sunlight; they are eaten by the Daphnia, and then, in turn, the Daphnia are eaten by the guppies. How many examples of this food chain can

the children supply? Are all living things a part of a food chain? Have fun with the children devising various food chains. Always remember the ultimate source: the sun.

This unit supplies experiences basic to all living things. Living things are born, they eat, they grow, they multiply, and then they die.

## Lesson 8

The individual aquaria are small ecological systems which demonstrate the basic concept of the food chain. An additional activity for this unit could be the production of microecological systems—microecology. The materials necessary are test tubes, green plants (Elodea), Daphnia, water, and stoppers.

Provide each child with a test tube, one green plant (Elodea), and one animal (Daphnia). Place the animal and green plant in the test tube with some water. Some children will use tap water, some distilled water, and others aquarium water. Encourage the use of different sources of water. Stopper the test tubes and seal with wax. Each child will then have a microecological system to observe in school, at home, or both.

Test tubes filled with aquarium water will "live" for a long time, while the others filled with tap water or distilled water will "die" rapidly. Can the children explain why? Hopefully they will relate their reasons to the food chain and its adequacy in each situation.

An interesting activity to conclude the formal part of this unit might be to make a ditto master on which certain plants and animals, and the sun, are sketched clearly labeled, and ask the children to show the food chain by drawing arrows between sketches. One such drawing might include the following: sun, water, Volvox, Daphnia, and guppies.

# HOT AND COLD

Young children have experienced the sensation of hot and cold (the absence of heat) many times in their daily activities. However, they know relatively little of the characteristics and causes of this form of energy.

Investigations designed to explore the effects of heat are the basis for this unit. Students are encouraged to experiment with this phenomenon by direct experiences.

## How to Begin

A way of informally initiating a unit involving an investigation of heat and heat effects might be to challenge the class to feel their wooden desk tops and describe whether they are warm or cold. Then have them touch the metal legs of their chairs or desks and compare the temperature there to that of the wooden portion. The majority will exclaim that the metal feels cooler. In reality, the wood and the metal are at the same temperature as the room, but the metal is a good conductor of heat and thus conducts the heat away from the children's hands rapidly, making them feel cooler. Much discussion can be generated from this one experiment and lead to an exchange of ideas on heat and cold. Begin by gathering the following simple materials in sufficient quantities: ice cubes, thermometers, paper cups, and metal spoons.

## Why Do It This Way?

A study of heat is generally overlooked with primary children for its effects are usually taken for granted, and if explored at all, it is generally investigated only in relationship to the daily weather and not as a phenomenon in itself, a form of energy.

Simple experiments in the area of "hot and cold" can be accomplished with surprising results

by young children if an awareness of the characteristics of heat is first aroused and it is approached *qualitatively* rather than *quantitatively*.

## How to Do It

### Lesson 1

After the activity in the How to Begin section has been tried, fill three pans with water. One should be fairly warm and the other made cold (by adding ice cubes to it) while the third is left at room temperature. Have a volunteer from the class place one hand in each of the pans marked warm and cold for about one minute. Let him describe his sensations. Now have the student put both hands in the pan of water kept at room temperature. The reaction of the child should be interesting. The hand previously immersed in the warm water and now plunged into the cooler (room temperature) water will feel cool. Conversely, the hand which had been placed in the cold water will now feel warm. This experiment should raise some questions concerning temperature. Allow the class to try variations of this investigation and relate them to experiences they may have had after playing in the snow and then entering a warm house. Do they recall the sensation of the cold tap water feeling warm?

## Lesson 2

This lesson involves exploring some of the many ways in which heat is generated. The following activities can be tried individually or in small groups.

*Friction:* Ask the children to rub their hands together vigorously and have them describe the results.

*Electricity:* Light an electric bulb. Have each child hold his hand close by. Let them experiment by placing their hands in different locations—under, over, and to the side of the bulb.

*Burning of fuels:* Strike a match and light a candle. Ask the class to describe what is happening.

*Chemical reaction:* This is really analogous to the previous activity but serves to illustrate that considerable heat can be generated by combining substances without producing an actual flame. Give each child a paper cup and a small amount of plaster of paris. Add a few ounces of water to each cup and have the children stir with a spoon or stick. There will be some surprise over the degree of heat that is produced by the reaction. A discussion of how the body "burns" food and produces the heat necessary for life functions may be initiated at this point.

*Solar radiation:* Give each student a small magnifying lens. Allow some time for free play and general exploration with the lens. If it doesn't occur naturally, suggest that each student try to focus the rays of sunlight to a spot. There will probably be many questions, for their range of experience with small hand lenses will be varied. Ask questions concerning the possible value of this kind of heat from the sun. Can it be used to cook food? (In India, solar furnaces are actually being used for cooking purposes since organic fuels are scarce.)

A discussion of how plants grow and use sunlight to manufacture food might develop from this activity. Further implications of "food chains" might well bring home the realization that the sun is the ultimate source of energy from which all life, either directly or indirectly, can be traced.

The following activities are simple investigations into the phenomenon of heat absorption.

1. Divide the class into teams of two and provide each team with two coffee cans or some other similar container and two thermometers. Have each team fill one can with water and the other with soil. Then have them insert a thermometer into each can and record the temperature level. Next, place the containers in the sun and have each team record the temperature again. Repeat hourly or as often as possible. Ask questions such as: Are the readings the same in each can? If they are different, why do you think this occurred? Which can be heated faster? Would there be any further difference if another type of soil was used? Try it and find out.

2. Repeat the same activity on another day but this time remove the cans from the sun after about three or four hours. Now record the cooling of both soil and water. How do they compare? Does one cool faster than the other?

3. Using the same containers, paint one black and the other white (or just peel or scrape the label off one, leaving the metal reflective surface). Remove the tops and cover each with a stiff piece of cardboard. Cut a small hole in the center of each piece of cardboard and insert a thermometer. Place both cans with thermometer in place outside in the sun and have each team record the temperature changes over a reasonable period of time. Which can warms up more quickly? Questions dealing with the types and color of clothing worn in different climates may be asked. Which color clothing dries the fastest on a clothesline, the dark or the light?

4. Using the same cans from the previous activity, try filling them with hot water. Cover with cardboard and insert the thermometer. Record the changing temperatures. Which cools faster?

5. Give each team a paper cup and one ice cube. Have one member of the team record the time while the other attempts to get the cube to melt. On the first try, restrict the teams from physically touching the ice cubes. The team that gets their cube to melt first is the winner. On the next try, allow the teams to handle the ice cubes. All kinds of interesting comments will develop from this activity. Variations involving different-shaped ice cubes frozen in cookie cutters and other odd-shaped household items may be used. Placing the

various-shaped "ice objects" on a piece of paper towel will produce intriguing patterns as the ice melts. (Usually the shape of the objects will be recorded or imprinted on the towel.) Another approach is to place the ice cubes in paper cups half filled with water. Does the water increase or retard the melting rate? Does the location of the cups affect the rate of melting? Does the volume of water influence the rate of melting? This activity is limited only by the enthusiasm and imagination of the students and teacher. In each case an exciting race among the teams can be instituted and will add a lot of interest to the experiment.

# MAGNETS

### How to Begin

"You can pick up things!" exclaims a primary child, and this becomes the start of the first formalized experience with magnets.

Probably the most universal difficulty experienced by primary teachers planning an activity on magnetism is the inadequate supply of magnets available for class activities. Magnets must be available in large quantity, with at least one bar magnet per child a minimum. Additional material for this first introduction to magnetism should include: paper clips, nails, washers, screws, pins, toothpicks, thumbtacks, corks, rubber bands, paper cups, paper plates, string, and various-shaped magnets.

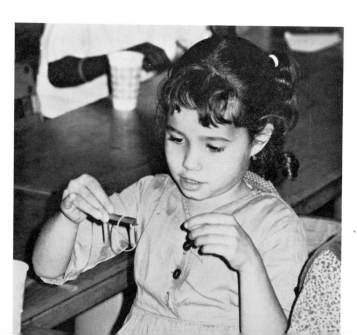

### Why Do It This Way?

Although at first we may not realize it, magnetic force is a new and startling kind of force to a child. It acts at a distance. Contact between objects is not necessary. Children are well acquainted with contact forces—pushes and pulls in the play yard, classroom, or halls—but a force which "acts through a distance" is not considered an ordinary part of their bumping, pushing, poking world.

The "up-down" orientation of our physical world results from our concept of gravity, which is also a force that "acts through a distance." Children may speak of gravity, but their concept of this effect (if they have one) is not customarily related to distance (most likely contact).

The main thrust of this unit is not the "acting at a distance" concept. Children at this level cannot fully appreciate the significance of this notion (there is no valid reason why they should) but possibly a beginning can be initiated by helping them to notice the distance feature. Children will be interested primarily in what objects the magnet can "affect." Thus, classification of objects affected and not affected by magnets should be of major concern.

### How to Do It

*Lesson 1*

The best way to begin a unit on magnets is to supply each child with one magnet and a small envelop containing paper clips, nails, and washers. Permit "aimless" play with the magnets. Do not direct attention to any one activity performed by various individuals. Listen to their comments while you note their self-directed activities. There will be a generous sharing of ideas and experiences.

While this activity is in process you might set up little demonstrations aimed at motivating increased interest in magnetic forces. Suspend a magnet (horseshoe or bar) from a support. Fasten a paper clip by a string (or black thread, to render it almost invisible) to the base of the support so that the clip will not touch the magnet. The paper clip remains suspended, attracted toward the magnet.

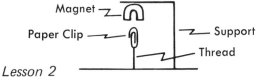

## Lesson 2

Activities with the magnets now become more directed. Suggest that the children make a record of things attracted or not attracted by a magnet. The teacher can supply a sample record sheet for collecting data. On the record sheet the first block is for drawing a picture of the object and in the adjacent two blocks the correct response, "yes" or "no," is circled. The teacher may have to demonstrate use of the record sheet.

Each child's supply of objects should be increased, including objects not attracted by magnets (corks, toothpicks). Paper cups or plates may be helpful to the children in keeping their objects all together.

*Record Sheet*

Picture of Object

| | YES | NO |
|---|---|---|
| | YES | NO |
| | YES | NO |
| | YES | NO |
| | YES | NO |
| | YES | NO |

## Lesson 3

Do magnets attract through things? Have children place objects on a piece of paper or card-

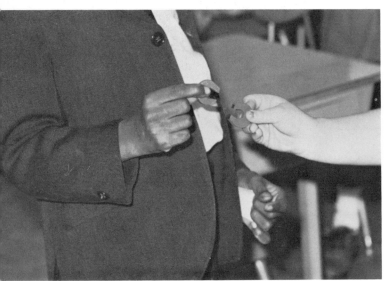

board and note how they can "move" these objects with the magnet. The magnet acts "through" the paper or cardboard. Possibly some child will express surprise over the observation that the magnet is not touching the object—yet it moves. Here may be the first opportunity to explain that not all forces are contact forces. Refer to the demonstration set up during the first lesson.

Various materials should be used in observing how the magnetic force acts through them. Try tap water. Place objects in a paper cup containing water. Does the magnet "work through" the water? Encourage children to use many combinations of materials.

### Lesson 4

Where is the magnet the strongest? Suggest that the children place their magnet in a cup filled with pins. Ask them to draw pictures of the magnet with the pins clinging to it. Question the children on their pictures. One generalization that can come from this question-discussion period will be that magnets seem to attract best "at their ends."

### Lesson 5

Can we make magnets? Can magnets be used to make other magnets? Supply each child with a couple of paper clips and a collection of straight pins. Have them straighten out their paper clips (demonstrate). Ask the children to "pick up the pins with the straight paper clip." Will the paper clips pick up the pins like a magnet does?

Now show the children how to magnetize their straight paper clips. Hold the magnet in one hand and stroke the paper clip in *one direction* thirty times. After the children do this, have them once again try to pick up the pins with the clip. Encourage the children to make magnets out of other objects. They will not be successful with all objects.

### Lesson 6

There are several additional activities which can be a part of any beginning unit on magnets. Some of them are:

96

1. Assemble a collection of different sizes and shapes of magnets.
2. Collect a display of toys using magnets.
3. Supply each child with a paper plate, glue, Saran wrap, and some iron filings. Place the iron filings in the paper plate and wrap the Saran wrap over the top of the plate. Glue around the edges. A magnet can now be placed under the plate and the various iron filing designs observed.
4. Try more activities with the demonstration developed in Lesson 1. How far away can the magnet be and still support the paper clip? Will various objects placed in the space between the magnet and paper clip affect the "pull" on the clip? Devise other demonstrations which feature the "force at a distance" concept.
5. Place a bar magnet under a piece of clear glass about the size of a windowpane. Place this arrangement on the surface of an overhead projector and sprinkle iron filings over the glass. A "beautiful" display of the field around the magnet can now be seen by all students.
6. Give each child a section cut from a waxed milk carton. Have them pass the carton sections over a candle flame briefly to soften the wax. Then, by placing a bar magnet underneath the piece of carton and sprinkling iron filings over the top while the wax is still warm, a permanent record of the magnetic field can be made when the wax hardens.

This unit emphasizes direct observation of what magnets can do. It is not concerned with terminology such as "poles," "north," "south," "like," "unlike," "lines of force" and "magnetic field." At this level none of these terms add any significant understanding to a youngster's early ideas about magnets and some of their characteristics.

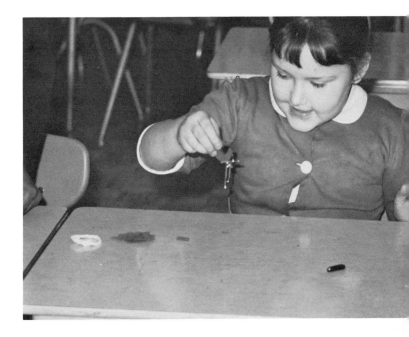

# MEASUREMENT FOR WEE PEOPLE

**How to Begin**

It has often been said that the tools with which man examines his environment are merely extensions of his perceptions. He scrutinizes the world of small things with the aid of a microscope and then turns his telescope lenses toward the heavens and searches the realm of the infinitely large.

As man continues to expand his reach and explores the bottom of the sea, the solar system, the interior of the earth, and the world of microscopic things he constantly compares the objects he observes with established norms of measurement. Young children, too, when exploring their own limited world, are confronted with similar situations. Measurement is such a big part of understanding basic concepts concerning numbers that it is imperative to expose students to some simple fundamentals of measurement as early as possible.

We should not be too concerned with merely teaching young children about inches, centimeters, pounds, or kilograms. Instead, we should attempt to introduce them to general relationships between size and weight.

If a child can cut a strip of construction paper equivalent to his height and compare it to strips cut by other members of his class, he can begin to get some sensation of relative differences in size.

The same can be done with units of weight. How big or how heavy something is takes on meaning only when we compare it against something else. This may also lead to the evolving of some simple concepts of graphing. Generally, in all measurement, man makes use of two basic rules. First it is necessary to have some uniform length or unit of weight to measure with; second, this must be compared with a known standard.

The history of measurement is filled with examples of how various units have been developed. Most were determined by rather arbitrary methods. But as long as everyone had access to the objects that were used and they were plentiful and could be compared to some reliable standard previously agreed upon, then the unit of measurement could serve a useful purpose. The development of standards is a very important consideration in obtaining an understanding of the history of measuring. Many units of length began as lengths of parts of the human body. The foot was based on the length of a man's foot, usually the reigning king's. The inch was the width of his thumb. The yard was the distance from his nose to the tips of the fingers of his outstretched arm. Even in ancient times it was realized that units of length could not be equal to the parts of just anyone's body. The lengths of men's arms, fingers, and feet differed from one person to another. It was decided that the units of length must be the same for everyone who wanted to use them. Similar sets of circumstances developed the units of weight.

**Why Do It This Way?**

This basic unit on measurement involves the use of simple materials and is designed to get children personally involved. In this way the discoveries they make will have a firm base and create a springboard for more sophisticated measurement studies as the child progresses through school. These lessons are not intended to last one period or session. Some may take a number of days. Let the class interest and enthusiasm serve as a guide for how much time is needed.

### How to Begin

#### Lesson 1

Materials needed: sheets of different-colored construction paper, scissors, paste or tape, a tack board or wall space on which to paste graphs, a bathroom scale, and a number of yardsticks or metersticks.

Begin by having each youngster cut a strip of construction paper an arbitrary length and suggest that they use the strips to measure various objects in the room. They might try measuring the length of the room, the width of their desks, the length of each other's arms, the circumference of classmates' heads, etc. Permit them to explore freely as many dimensions as possible using their newly constructed measuring tools. Many questions will arise such as: "Do we all need the same size strip?" or "Mary's paper is longer than mine. Why?" The teacher should encourage the children to exchange ideas with others in the class. They will probably compare their results with their neighbors and be somewhat puzzled when their measurements for the same objects do not match up. An interesting variation might be tried by asking some children to use an "elastic" or long piece of rubber for their measuring device. This activity will serve as a good launching point into subsequent lessons where a standard unit of measurement is used and the results are more tangible.

Still another area of measurement, temperature, can be investigated. A large thermometer in the classroom can be used to stimulate interest. Assign members of the class the responsibility of reading and recording the temperature. A simple but effective facsimile of a thermometer can also be constructed from a piece of oak tag and a large loop of elastic, half of which has been colored

red. By passing it through slots at the top and bottom of a scale inscribed on the surface, the simulated thermometer can then be adjusted by pulling the elastic up or down on the reverse side. If an indoor-outdoor thermometer can be obtained, students can make comparisons of the temperature in the classroom with that outside. Each day's temperature might be recorded on a list and placed where everyone can see it. The children may try to guess what the temperature will be. They will begin to associate a rise in temperature from morning through the early afternoon as the sun's energy warms the earth.

In the early fall, bring in a bathroom scale and some measuring sticks. Start the classroom discussion by asking the class if anyone knows how tall he is or how much he weighs. Children usually have very vague ideas about how tall they are or how much they weigh (in terms of feet or pounds). On the other hand, they can readily see that one youngster is taller or bigger (heavier) than another. Someone might volunteer the notion of using a scale. The teacher can display various objects of different weights and volume, and

ask the children to try and decide which one is heaviest. Again children are easily confused when an object of the same weight is merely changed in shape. This can be illustrated with a piece of clay. Cut a quarter of a pound of plasticene clay into a cube and flatten another quarter of a pound into a disc. Ask the children which is heavier. The results may prove surprising.

### Lesson 2

Weigh each youngster in the class and record the reading. A bathroom scale with a magnifying glass window over the numbers should prove helpful in letting the children read the figures for themselves.

Cut some strips of red construction paper into ten-inch lengths. These strips will be used to represent ten pounds each. Using blue paper, make strips five inches long to equal five pounds. Last, cut a sufficient number of strips of yellow paper to one-inch lengths to represent one-pound units. (The teacher should explain this to the class.)

A teacher who has been using cuiseniere rods might want to have the colors match the units for

one, ten, and five with those of the rods for quicker association by the class.

After weighing each child, give each one the appropriate strips of paper equivalent to his weight. Better still, allow the youngster to select the proper colors and quantities to represent his weight.

For example: If a child weighed 47 pounds he would receive or select

| | | |
|---|---|---|
| four pieces of red paper | (4 X 10 = 40 pounds) | |
| one piece of blue paper | (1 X 5 = 5 pounds) | |
| two pieces of yellow paper | (2 X 1 = 2 pounds) | |
| | Total weight | 47 pounds |

Assist the students in joining their strips to form one long strip representative of their total weight, using Scotch tape, paste, or staples. Have each child write his name and the date the weight was recorded on his strip of paper. After weighing all the children ask them if they have any ideas for displaying or mounting their strips. Their suggestions will be many and varied. Try not to regulate the methods suggested. Hopefully, someone will suggest the possibility of pasting their strips on the bulletin board or wall. Interesting discussion can be generated as the children devise different ways of displaying their strips. One outcome may be an arrangement in some sort of graph form. Do not be discouraged if this does not happen immediately. With proper direction and guidance and a willingness to be patient most classes will gravitate in this direction.

### Lesson 3

This same approach can be used toward the measurement of the height of each youngster. It is not necessary to have individual units representing specific quantities. One long strip or a combination of strips of one color equaling the height of each child will do. A different color for each student will prove attractive and possibly aid as means of identification. This same activity—the measurement of height and weight—should be repeated in late spring. In this way the class can see some rather conspicuous changes in the positions they occupy in the growth graph of their class. From an activity such as this, children are exposed to basic concepts of measurement involving their own bodies. They are given a chance to visualize growth changes in their bodies and relate them to the changes experienced by other members of the class. Fundamental concepts of relative differences in length and weight can be brought closer to the young child's level of understanding by getting him personally involved. By not being concerned with exact units of measurement but instead with relationships between large and small, light and heavy, long and short, this goal can be accomplished.

### Lesson 4

In this lesson many variations involving linear measurement and weight relationships can be explored. The ingenious teacher may delve into new areas in which simple materials can be utilized to permit children an opportunity to see a pattern to ways of measuring. Remember, all that is needed to make an effective measurement is something to compare with whatever it is you are attempting to measure, and, secondly, to compare your measurement with some known standard. Some examples of other methods that can be tried follow:

1. Have each child trace his hand on a piece of heavy oak tag and then cut out a number of these tracings. He now has a fixed unit to work with and can try measuring all kinds of objects in the room by placing his "hand units" from thumb to little finger in a line.
2. The same thing can be done with cutouts of shoe soles. Keep in mind that their unit of measurement is good only for their particular hand or foot cutouts.

Another exciting area of measurement can be explored by purchasing some commercial devices made specifically for children, which include everything from large calipers to graphs and scales (see section titled "Where to Find Out").

### Lesson 5

Materials needed: a quarter pound of plastic clay for each child and prepared worksheets.

This lesson can be used optionally or as a cul-

minating activity. In this lesson children are given a chance to investigate the relationship between weight and volume described earlier in this unit.

Give each child a quarter pound of clay and a copy of the worksheet. The teacher can make a basic shape, such as a cube or a sphere, from her piece of clay and have the students follow suit.

**101**

Then squash the piece into an amorphous form. After having the students do likewise, ask them to check the appropriate box on their worksheets.

If they think the object is now heavier they should check "elephant" for heavy. If their choice is lighter they should check the column headed by the "dog." If they think that there is no change, they should mark the last box, headed by the equal-sign.

| Shape | Heavy  | Light  | Equal |
|---|---|---|---|
| 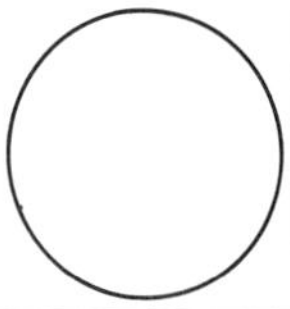 ⬤ | | | |
| 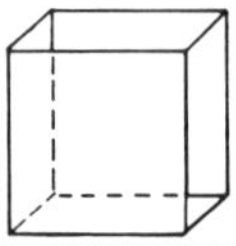 ▱ (cube) | | | |
|  ▭ | | | |
| 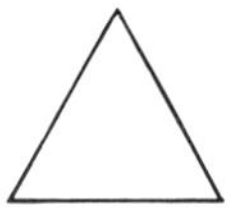 △ | | | |

# PLANTS WITHOUT SUNLIGHT

A mold is like a tiny plant. Unlike green plants, it does not make its own food. Given the proper environmental conditions of food, temperature, and moisture it will grow well. Children have used or heard the word "mold." Many have probably seen moldy bread, or other foods that have begun to spoil.

**How to Begin**

Collect cookie tins or shoe boxes (lined with aluminum foil). Any flat, broad container is adequate. There should be at least one container for each two or three children. Place a layer of soil (one inch deep) in each container. Use soil from

102

different places and keep a record of where the soil was obtained. Place pieces of leather, rubber, and plastic (two inches in size) on top of the soil in each container. The individual pieces should not be touching. Moisten the soil lightly (too much water will exclude all the air). Cover the container (a plastic "see-through" cover) tightly and position it in a warm place.

### Why Do It This Way?

Children will discover some of the growth characteristics of molds. Comparisons can be made between plants they know (flowers, etc.) and the growing molds. What are the similarities and differences? What is the life cycle of a mold? Is it like that of animals and plants? This unit should motivate the formulation of many questions about living things.

It is not difficult to grow molds. Children will become involved in an activity which can be related to experiences outside the classroom. Many children have seen moldy bread and possible wondered what is the origin of the "white-black stuff." Early understandings of variables and controls, as applied to experimentation, can result from the activities in this unit. As is true of all these units a major goal is to stimulate curiosity with the result that children will be motivated to formulate their own experimental procedures.

### How to Do It

Before proceeding to the use of the broad containers it is best to introduce this unit with a discussion and a class demonstration. The discussion may center around the proper storage of food and what things the children believe will happen to food when it is improperly stored.

As a demonstration, place a few pieces of bread in a closed, damp, warm place. Also place some bread in a closed, dry, cool place (this is the control). Get the children to discuss why they think two samples were set up in this demonstration. Accept their responses and do not be too eager to change or shape their answers. The class will observe this demonstration for a week or more. Soon mold will appear on the bread in the

closed, damp, warm environment. Children will make comparisons between the two samples.

The result of this demonstration will not be an understanding of what molds are, but simply the knowledge that some "white-black stuff" grows on bread when it is stored in a closed, damp, warm place. Certain general questions will direct class activities toward other experiments which will lead to more understanding of molds. Where does the mold come from? Was it already in the bread? (both difficult questions). Will other things "grow" molds? What other things? Do molds "grow" in soil like plants?

Mold is a tiny plant which must live on food made by other plants or animals, or on decaying matter. Molds have no chlorophyll and therefore cannot manufacture their own food. They are "plants without sunlight."

Molds belong to the fungi groups and develop from tiny particles called spores. These spores are usually microscopic and of many different types

produced in enormous numbers by parent bodies and distributed far and wide by wind, water, and animals.

When the spore settles on some damp food such as bread, it swells and begins to grow by producing tiny threads (hyphae). As the mold matures more spores are produced and set free to be carried away by air currents. Common bread molds are a soft, cottony, white growth. Some bread molds are called "black molds," so named because these molds produce dark-colored spores. There is a group of "blue molds" which grow on bread. Green molds are usually observed on various kinds of cheeses.

Now construct the broad containers and get the children to bring in their samples of soil. Set them up as indicated earlier

Soils contain many species of molds, which feed on the organic material in the soil. The plastic, rubber, and leather pieces represent three possible

sources of food for the molds. The molds will grow well on the leather, ignore the plastic, and grow a little bit on the rubber.

Because leather is organic in origin it will be digested by molds. The other items will be more resistant to molds.

This experiment can lead to additional ones. Try different kinds of leather, plastic, or rubber—in fact, try any items the children want to use. During their experimentation you may have to remind the class about the "control" you used in the bread experiment. Children working in teams set up two situations: items in a closed, moist, warm container and the same items in a closed, dry, cool container. What comparisons become apparent?

The experimenting can also include manipulating the "variables." Try situations in which two containers with the same items are both in a warm place, but one moist and the other dry; or, both in a warm place and one moist and one dry but neither one covered. Many combinations are possible. Given the opportunity, the children will suggest most of them. The teacher's major roll in these activities is assisting the class to organize all the collected information from these experiments.

Work with molds need not end here. Children may become interested in knowing more about them and their observed effect on foods. Possibly this was already started earlier in the unit because of class or individual interest. This unit is open-ended and provides considerable opportunity for children to engage in the "process of science."

# PLANTING SEEDS

### How to Begin

Living things are always of interest to primary children. How do plants grow? Where do they grow? Do all plants look alike? Do people eat plants?

Plants come from seeds, so begin this unit by first obtaining a large collection of different seeds, some soil, and appropriate containers (half pint paper milk cartons are excellent). A hand magnifying glass should also be available for each child.

### Why Do It This Way?

Through discussions about plants, motivated by student activities, certain common features of all plants will be observed. These features, such as root, stem, and leaf, are easily classified in most plants and thus permit further practice in the technique of identification and classification. The materials required for this unit are easily obtained and can yield months of enjoyment for the children.

### How to Do It

Obtain an abundant collection of seeds. A suggested assortment is: one half pound of Indian corn, one half pound of yellow corn, one half pound of dried peas, a quarter pound of radish seeds, and one pound of lima beans. Most seed stores will have seeds available in bulk quantities. These are preferable to the small packages available in various stores. Soil can be obtained from home, around the school yard, or purchased in twenty-pound bags from hardware stores.

Provide each child with a collection of various seeds. Do not identify the seeds for the children. Let them identify the seeds with which they are familiar. Some may not be familiar with any of the seeds. Some children may not even recognize the "objects" as seeds. Listen to the comments made by the children. Encourage them to describe their seeds: how they feel, look, smell. Examine the seeds by cutting them open; soak the hard ones in water.

The children probably will want to plant their seeds. Make the soil and cartons available in large numbers (three or four cartons per child) and then control your desire to direct "how the seeds should be planted." Some seeds will be planted too deep, others just on or below the surface of the soil or next to the side of the container. Some children will use too much soil, others too little. Some will use too much water as well as insist on frequent watering.

Youngsters should label their cups with their names and the type seed planted in each. Provide material for labeling (Scotch tape and strips of

construction paper). Inform the children that this material is "here for labeling," but do not indicate a procedure on how to label. Some children will write the name of the seed on the outside of the cup (assuming they know the name); others will tape a sample of the seed on the outside of the cup; while still others will draw a picture, on the outside of the cup, of the seed planted. Any procedure that is meaningful to the child should be accepted.

Because each child will ultimately have three, four, or five separate containers it is suggested that they bring to school shoe boxes in which to keep their collection of small cartons. If children are permitted to have the number of plants here suggested, a major problem will be finding places to keep all the plants, Experience, however, has indicated that the space problem created by this large collection of plants is more than offset by the class enthusiasm generated by the freedom of activity in this unit. In other words, live with a difficult logistics problem—it's worth it.

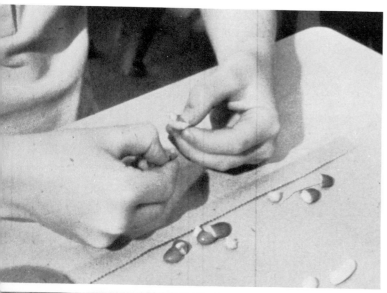

Soon after the children have planted their seeds some may be unable to contain their curiosity and will dig up the seeds. They want to see if "anything is happening." This may happen only minutes, hours, or a day after the actual planting. Do not discourage children from doing this; rather, listen to their expressions of disappointment because "nothing has happened."

After several days most of the seeds will be planted and the children will have selected "good spots" to keep their collection of cartons. At this point suggest that each child start a "record of events sheet." This can be placed next to the plants and such things as watering times, amount of daylight, observation of first "shoot," and growth (measurement) of plant can be tabulated as the days go by.

After several days have passed you might encourage children to dig up one of their seeds (in some classes this suggestion will be unnecessary). The seed can be replanted and probably will develop normally. Observations of this sort will reveal the first "shoot" extending out of the seed into the soil. As the seed develops it will be noted that the "seed covering" has cracked and is later discarded. For all observations a hand magnifying glass should be available to each child.

Soon the individual plants will begin to flourish. Stems will develop and then will come leaf formations. These should be closely observed and the "running record" maintained. As the plant develops, once again encourage "digging"—only this time dig up the root to view its structure. Use the hand magnifiers to obtain a closer view of the hairlike roots. The plant can be replanted and in all probability it will continue to survive. The plants will grow rapidly and this should lead logically to measuring activities. The measuring instrument can be construction paper strips or a ruler. Various procedures will be used in keeping track of growth. Try to encourage a regularity in the children's measuring activities as well as some method of recording the information.

Planting things and observing plants growing can be an all-year activity. Specific activities are suggested in this unit. These activities should serve as a beginning from which "growing things" will become a regular, on-going, year-round process.

# ROCK SORTING

Young children enjoy collecting and classifying many different kinds of things. Rocks are a good example of a material readily available in most areas and may serve as a means of opening up ways for primary youngsters to categorize and name various rock specimens in an approach that is creative and integrates the subjects of art and science.

## How to Do It

The teacher may start this unit by posing a riddle to the class: "There is an object many millions of years old in this classroom. What do you think it is?" Allow the children to guess freely. (They probably won't make the association that the blackboard is actually very old rock. Slate, which is used for traditional blackboards, is a type of metamorphic rock.) A great deal of discussion may develop from this one question. Newer schools may not have real slate blackboards. A sample of slate may be obtained from the local lumberyard.

On the next day the teacher should take the class for a short field trip around the school grounds to collect rocks. If a natural area abundant in rocks is lacking near the school, the teacher may ask the children to bring some from home, or as a *last* resort they may be ordered from a scientific supply house. Whatever the source, try to get as much variety as possible. The size of the rock specimens should be kept relatively small.

## Why Do It This Way?

Young children are usually quite interested in identifying rocks or stones that they have picked up. How often has a young child asked you such questions as: "Where do rocks come from?" or "What kind of rock is this?" or "What is the shiny stuff in this rock?" More often than not the teacher has to admit to not knowing the answer and generally decides that the ability to identify a particular mineral or a combination of minerals in a rock should be left to trained mineralogists and is beyond the capacity of young students. On the contrary, children are very astute at observing differences and similarities in objects, and rocks and minerals are no exception. Simple tests can be utilized. Opportunities to explore properties of texture, color, size, volume, density, and weight will be available as the children attempt to identify their rocks. Primary children will, of course, make many mistakes in their attempts to name and classify their specimens and in many instances may not be able to identify them at all. Accept these limitations, for similar problems face trained scientists daily in their laboratories. Children need confrontations and experiences in which they occasionally do not succeed completely or come up with "right answers."

## How to Do It

### Lesson 1

Materials needed: one empty egg carton per student, magnifying glasses, one set of representative rock specimens. Each youngster should also have his own cigar box filled with different kinds of rocks.

Ask the children to group together all rocks that look alike. Try to get them to separate as many different kinds of rocks as possible. Allow them to use any characteristic that they can devise. Some may choose color, others texture or size. Let each youngster determine which criteria he will use. It is not as difficult as one may think. There are many excellent reference books containing large pictures that the children can use to compare their specimens (see *"Where to Find Out"* section). Do not be too concerned with the degree of accuracy achieved. The method of investigating and attempting to classify by using references, experimenting, and just raising questions may be more important than right answers.

When a child feels that a specific "rock" has been identified, suggest that he place it in one of the cups of the egg carton and label it.

### Lesson 2

Materials needed: pennies, file, piece of glass, ten penny nails.

A simple scale of "hardness" is another method which can be used to aid the students in classifying their mineral specimens. This scale is often referred to as the Moh Scale of Hardness. Substances are rated on this scale of relative hardness from 1 to 10, with diamond listed as the hardest substance and given a value of 10.

Remember, these tests are specifically for *minerals*, and rocks are composed of two or more minerals. This may result in some confusion when the children try to "nail" down each specimen. Again, allow latitude in the identities they assign as long as the techniques and approach they use appear sound.

### Moh Scale of Hardness

10  Diamond—can scratch all other substances listed below it
9  Corundum (Ruby)
8  Topaz—nothing approximate for comparison to hardness
7  Quartz—scratches glass easily
6  Orthoclase (feldspar)—scratched by a file
5  Apatite—not scratched easily by a ten-penny nail

4　Fluorite—scratched easily by a ten-penny nail

3　Calcite—cut easily by knife, scratched slightly by penny

2　Gypsum—can be scratched by fingernail

1　Talc—soft, greasy, flakes on fingers (used to make bath powder)

The hardness of a mineral can be determined by scratching it with a known substance (fingernail 2.5, penny 3, glass 5.5, a ten-penny nail 5.5, file 6.5). Some children may devise scales of their own, using other objects as a standard for hardness. Encourage as much originality as possible.

### Lesson 3

Materials needed: sample mineral specimens from a commercial kit, pieces of unglazed bathroom or porcelain tile.

Streak is the mark that a particular mineral makes when rubbed on the back of a piece of bathroom tile or a commercial streak plate. This test will indicate whether the specimen is a metallic or nonmetallic mineral. Metals will make a dark green, dark brown, gray, or black streak. Nonmetals will make colorless or white streaks. The teacher can make a large chart indicating this color code, and the youngsters can try to duplicate the colors by the use of crayons.

### Lesson 4

This investigation can prove to be one of the most exciting in the unit if time and interest are sufficient.

Many rocks do not exhibit their true wonder and beauty on their outside surfaces. Usually weathering and dirt mar the appearance. Washing the rocks helps but still does not "show off" the internal structure of the specimen. Try covering a large rock with a towel or piece of cloth. Place it on a solid flat surface and strike it with a hammer. It normally doesn't take much force to split or fracture the rock. Have the class examine the surface of the rock broken in this manner. There is usually a vast difference in texture and coloration. If fieldstone is available around the school, interesting samples can be examined and com-

pared by this method. A sample array of such broken rocks can be identified and displayed in class and the children may compare their new-found collections with these. Encourage the children to make charts of their rock specimens. This can be done individually or by the entire class.

## Lesson 5

A beginning understanding of density can be initiated by asking the children to "heft" their rock specimens and to attempt some classification by weight. Also, samples of rocks can be soaked in

water overnight to see if some will absorb more water than others. Both of these investigations can lead to questions concerning porosity as well as density, weight, and volume.

Last, some specimens can be reacted with vinegar (acetic acid) or some other weak acid. Those that "fizz" contain carbonates. Practically all of those that "fizz" will be either calcite (the mineral), limestone, or marble (the rock).

## Lesson 6

The following activity should provide an exciting climax for the rock-classifying project. By this time most of the class will have identified or at least grouped similar "rock-mineral" specimens together. Ask if they can see any interesting shapes or figures in some of the collections. Suggest that they group specimens together and try to make little men or animals of their rocks. Paint can be added to enhance or embellish a particular design. Children will have a great deal of fun in creating their little rock animals and men. They can glue the pieces together when a satisfactory arrangement has been achieved and then paste their design on a piece of oak tag. When this has been accomplished they can consult their list of mineral names and assign names such as Mr. Feldspar, Mrs. Granite, Mr. Mica Schist, Bunny Shale, and Chicken Sandstone to their creation.

## Special Background Information for the Teacher

The following section has been included to aid the teacher in working with her students as they attempt to identify and name the rocks they will be collecting.

Rocks are grouped into three types: (1) sedimentary, (2) igneous, and (3) metamorphic.

(1) Sedimentary rocks are formed from sediments or fragments of other rocks which have been cemented together. Sediments come from rocks broken down by the process of weathering. The action of the sun's heat, rain, frost, running water (rivers,

streams, etc.), and wind are factors of weathering. These sediments are carried by water, wind, streams, etc., and deposited in the bottoms of lakes, oceans, rivers, and ponds. Tons of this material are squeezed and cemented by the solutions in the water (carbonate of potassium, sodium, magnesium, calcium, iron, etc., together with sulfates and chlorides). Some examples of sedimentary rocks follow. One is sandstone (grindstone), which is sand cemented together. Conglomerate has gravel, sand, and pebbles cemented. Shale is cemented mud, silt, and clay. Salt is a chemical precipitate. Limestone (chalk-dolomite) is the remains of animals (bones, shells, etc.).

(2) Igneous rock is often a dark, dense rock that is formed deep within the earth. Generally known as "fire rock" because of its molten or liquid state (called magma), it is believed to be the oldest kind of rock. Due to extreme heat and tremendous pressure, magma has a tendency to work its way throug' other rocks (sedimentary, metamorphic, a ther igneous rock) and may erupt on the face, forming a volcano. As the magma reaches the surface (called extrusive igneous rock) it cools quickly. Little crystallization occurs and/or very fine grained crystals result because of the rapid cooling (for example, basalt). Magma that cools within the interior of the crust is known as intrusive igneous rock (plutonic rock). The crystals are larger because of slow cooling (for example, granite). Other examples of igneous rock are pumice, obsidian, porphyry, syenite, and granite.

(3) Metamorphic or "changed rock" is sedimentary and igneous rock that has been changed due to folding, warping, compression, and heat. Recrystallization occurs in the minerals of this rock. Examples of metamorphic rocks that have been changed are:

Shale changed to slate (blackboard in classroom is a good example)
Conglomerate changed to quartzite

Sandstone changed to quartzite
Limestone changed to marble
Anthracite changed to graphite
Basalt changed to schist
Granite changed to gneiss

Rocks are made up of minerals. A mineral is an element or a combination of elements found naturally and must be inorganic. Granite is an igneous rock composed mainly of four mineral groups—quartz, feldspar, the amphiboles, and the micas. To identify or recognize minerals, tests must be made. Common minerals are classified by physical properties such as luster, color, hardness, crystal form, specific gravity, chemical com-

position, streak, cleavage, and fracture. Other means of identifying are magnetism, electrical properties, fluorescence, radioactivity. temperature of fusion, and optical properties.

Most of these tests are beyond the range of abilities and interests of young students but may aid the teacher in developing additional ways to challenge the class. The lessons in this unit are based upon the kinds of tests and activities which children *can* perform in classifying their rock specimens.

*A Rocks and Minerals Key to*
*Assist the Teacher*

(A key is a device used to identify objects, animals, plants, etc., by salient characteristics. Usually these characteristics can be readily observed by their physical properties of color, texture, size, weight, taste, shape, etc.)

Materials needed: piece of glass, streak plate (back of unglazed bathroom tile), paper, file.

This key is designed to help you identify certain rocks and minerals. It does not work for all rocks and minerals, and only the following list of representative specimens can be identified with this key. This key is designed in couplets. Each couplet is numbered and asks specific questions (such as in 1a, 1b, 2a, 2b, etc.).

(a)   obsidian
(b)   coal
(c)   tar
(d)   pyrite
(e)   graphite
(f)   mica
(g)   slate or shale
(h)   sandstone
(i)   garnet
(j)   chalk
(k)   calcite
(l)   quartz
(m)   feldspar

*How to Use This Key*

Examine a rock specimen and ask yourself the questions in couplet number 1a, 1b. If the answer is positive proceed to couplet number 2a, 2b. If the answer is negative proceed to couplet 15a, 15b. Continue to follow this system until the specimen is identified.

*KEY*

1a  Is dark in color ____2____ .

1b  Is *not* dark in color ____15____ .

2a  Is black in color as opposed to being gray, red, or tan ____3____ .

2b  Is *not* black in color but is gray, red, or dark tan ____7____ .

3a  Has a hardness of about 5.5 ____6____ .

3b  Has a harndess of less than 5.5 ____4____ .

4a  Makes a black mark on the streak plate ____5____ .

4b  Makes a mark other than black on the streak plate ____5____ .

5a  Has a distinct smell _____ (tar).

5b  Has no apparent odor or smell ____6____ .

6a  Has sharp glasslike edges _____ (obsidian).

6b  Has no sharp edges _____ (coal).

7a  Is gray or yellow in color ____8____ .

7b  Is brown or reddish in color ____11____ .

8a  Is soft with hardness less than 2.2 ____9____ .

8b  Is harder than 2.2 ____10____ .

9a  Has a greasy feel ____10____ .

9b  Does not have a greasy feel ____10____ .

10a  Crystals visible, producing black streak _____ (pyrite crystals).

10b  Crystals small, insignificant, producing black streak _____ (graphite).

11a  Has apparent layers or shows stratification ____12____ .

11b  No apparent layers or uneven cleavage ____13____ .

12a Cleavage in layers or sheets—layers are semi-transparent or translucent _____ (mica).

12b Cleavage in layers—layers are not transparent or translucent _____ (slate or shale).

13a Harndess more than 6.5 __14__ .

13b Hardness about 6.5 __14__ .

14a Sandy texture—no visible crystals _____ (sandstone or grindstone).

14b Glassy, or glasslike with many sides, isometric system _____ (garnet crystal).

15a White in color __16__ .

15b Not completely white, but pinkish, tan, or or smoky in color __19__ .

16a Has hardness more than 5.5 __19__ .

16b Has hardness less than __17__ .

17a Produces white streak on plate _____ (chalk or dolomite).

17b No streak made on plate __18__ .

18a Has hardness less than 2.5 _____ (chalk).

18b Has hardness of about 3.0 _____ (calcite crystal).

19a Crystals apparent—6-sided _____ (quartz crystal).

19b No apparent crystals visible __20__ .

20a Tan or pink in color _____ (feldspar).

20b White or glasslike _____ (quartz crystal).

# SHADOWS AND SUNDIALS

### How to Begin

A simple yet very rewarding activity can center around shadows. As an introduction you might read aloud "My Shadow" by Robert Louis Stevenson.

Assemble necessary materials such as: filmstrip projector, screen, small flashlights (one for each two children), styrofoam balls (two sizes, 2-inch and 1-inch), clay, shoe boxes, and pencils (or dowels). These materials will be used by the children to experiment with shadows. Individual or small group activity should be emphasized.

### Why Do It This Way?

Early notions about light and the shadows cast by various objects will be developed in this unit. Children will realize that an object's shape and its shadow are related and that the size and shape of a shadow changes with the location of the object and the position of the light source.

**How to Do It**

Suggested activities for this unit have been divided into lessons. A single lesson should continue for as long as there is class interest in the activity. Each lesson does not represent one science class period.

### Lesson 1

Set up a screen and filmstrip projector in the room. Permit children to make shadows with their hands or other objects. Listen to their explanations about the shadows they make. Do not be too eager to direct their activities.

### Lesson 2

Organize the class into pairs. Supply each pair with a shoe box containing some clay, a small flashlight, and a pencil. Initially, simply observe what the children do with these materials. Possibly the experiences from the first activity with the filmstrip projector will motivate children to use these materials in "play with shadows."

The pencil can be supported in the shoe box by sticking it in the piece of clay. The flashlight can then be used, from various angles, to produce "pencil shadows." Make some record—visible to all the children—of all the observations resulting from this activity.

### Lesson 3

Set up the filmstrip projector and screen. Position a child between the projector and the screen. Question the class about the location and size of the shadow as the child moves to different positions. Is the shadow always directly behind the child? When is the shadow largest? When does the shadow move? Note that all children are viewing the shadow from different locations in the room: how does this affect their responses?

### Lesson 4

Return to the shoe box with the pencil, the clay, and the flashlight. Ask the children how shadows can be made long or short. Changing the position of the pencil or flashlight or both will result in various-length shadows. Activities suggested by the pencil and flashlight can be reproduced using the filmstrip projector and screen.

### Lesson 5

Provide each pair with one large and one small styrofoam ball. Once again set up the filmstrip projector and screen. Observe how the children use the balls to make shadows (no doubt these balls will be suggestive of other activities). This activity can also be performed using the flashlights. Can a shadow of one ball hide the shadow of the other? Are all shadows dark? Can some shadows become light? Do two objects have to be touching in order for their shadows to touch? These and many other questions can stimulate exciting discussions.

### Lesson 6

A simple screen can be constructed by suspending a bed sheet from the ceiling. Place the filmstrip projector on one side of the screen with the screen positioned between the children and the projector. Place various objects behind the screen and let the children try to identify each object from its shadow.

Make a collection of cardboard shapes—triangles, circles, squares, rectangles—and experiment with the identification of these shapes from the shadows they cast. Some experience can be

gained using three-dimensional objects such as cones, spheres, pyramids, cubes, and cylinders. Young children have had little experience identifying two- and three-dimensional shapes. Let them examine these shapes before you demonstrate some of the interesting shadows they cast.

### Lesson 7

Encourage children to make various objects to place behind the "bed sheet" screen. This can become a game of identification.

Finally, go out into the play yard and examine the many shadows provided by nature. It may be wise to refer again to the poem "My Shadow" by Robert Louis Stevenson. Possibly the recent experiences with shadows will make its content more meaningful to the children as well as stimulate further questions.

### Lesson 8

One of the most fascinating activities involving shadows is the construction of a sundial, through which a fundamental understanding of time can be gained by the children. The concept of time is often a much neglected area in school curricula. Primary youngsters in particular have difficulty in conceiving of time, for it is rather an abstract term.

Having used many different objects in the previous lessons of this unit, including parts of their bodies, for casting shadows, the class should now be prepared for something a bit more sophisticated.

Since earliest times man, like other creatures in his environment, was content to let his internal biological clock awake him at dawn and suggest sleep at dusk. As his food habits changed and he became more agrarian the establishment of a noon or midday meal was instituted. Food was now more readily available and he was no longer dependent upon food that was discovered here and there. He indicated noon as the time when the shadows lay midway between those of sunrise and sunset. Later, as primitive man attempted to influence his environment through ritual and incantations, he further divided the morning and afternoon into periods dedicated to the gods.

The earliest sundials were actually used to mark the intervals of time for such prayer. These interesting devices utilized the rotation of the earth on its axis to tell time.

Let us imagine that the surface of the earth is completely transparent and the axis is real and opaque. The sun would then cast the shadow of the axis on the far inner side of the earth. Then, as the earth turned, the shadow would remain fixed. To someone on the surface moving along with respect to the axis it would appear as though it was moving and completing a cycle every twenty-four hours. Thus, it would move fifteen degrees in one hour and one degree every four minutes.

There are many sundials similar to models of the earth that function in a manner similar to that described above. A good example of this is the statue of Atlas supporting an open sphere in front of the Radio City Building in New York. A less sophisticated sundial and one just as interesting can be constructed with simple materials by upper primary youngsters.

All that is needed is some construction paper or shirt cardboards, soda straws, pencils or crayons, and a simple compass.

Sundials can be very sophisticated and quite complicated, but in an activity for young children we are concerned primarily with exposing them to some basic ideas of how man uses the sun to determine time.

## Outdoor Activity

The teacher might begin by encouraging youngsters to use their own bodies as the centerpiece (style or gnomon) of a sundial and suggest that they attempt to try to find out where to stand in order to cast a shadow.

Questions such as Where is the sun? Is it north, south, east, or west? Where does your shadow point if the sun is in the east, south, west? Can anyone think of a way in which we can guess what time of day it is by looking at our shadows? When are shadows the longest? When are shadows the shortest? In what general direction do we have to look to see the sun? Does anyone know why? Do people in other parts of the world have to look in this direction to see the sun?

Responses will probably be quite varied depending upon the age and experience of the children.

If someone doesn't suggest that shadows might be used to indicate the time of day, the teacher may challenge the class with a question to this effect: Can we tell time by the movement of the sun?

A very simple sundial can be constructed by young children if only gross concepts of time intervals are dealt with. For example, by association with actual time on a school clock or a wristwatch, youngsters can become sensitive to the length and direction of a shadow cast by a stick or twig stuck in the ground. Perhaps a large circle can be described on the ground outside the classroom or in a school yard. The children are then given an opportunity to check the position and length of the shadow at different times of the day and are encouraged to record this information. At one school a teacher ingeniously used the shadow of the chain-link fence facing the school wall outside her room. The children marked the height of the shadow cast by the fence a few times each day and during different periods of the year. In this way the children got a feeling for not only short intervals of time but seasons as well.

Some youngsters may wish to construct small, portable sundials, a project that requires more serious investigation than might be appropriate at this level. However, do not discourage them if they wish to try. Problems associated with the orientation of the numbers of the dial (twelve o'clock should coincide with true north) and adjustments that have to be made in the angle of the gnomon or style (the object which casts the shadow at the center of the dial) will be too difficult for most primary children to solve.

The interested teacher can consult a number of references that deal with the mechanics of constructing a functional sundial, or the simple one described below can be tried.

A lone tree standing in a field suggests itself as a natural gnomon for a sundial, but it will not be very accurate. The slanting pointer, or gnomon, of a sundial points almost directly to the North Star (Polaris). Since the north end of the earth's axis points almost directly to the North Star a stick standing straight up would make a fine gnomon. But since we live on the curve of the earth's surface, some distance from the North Pole, you will need to slant the stick at an angle equal to the latitude of the location of your school. This information can be obtained from most maps or by calling the local library.

*Building a Sundial from*
*Simple Materials*

1. Open up a paper clip as illustrated in the drawing and insert the smaller of the two loops into the end of a five-inch length of straw.

2. Draw a circle of approximately twelve inches in diameter on a piece of oak tag or a shirt cardboard. Cut it in half and use each section for the base of a sundial.

3. Insert the larger loop of the paper clip through the slits marked A and B. Then bend the clip to the proper angle so the soda straw acts as a pointer.

4. Set your sundial on the ground or on a flat surface and point the gnomon at true north. North can be found by using a magnetic compass, but it will have to be corrected for true north. The teacher can establish a mark for true north by sighting the North Star through the straw pointer. Keep a record of its position on the ground for the next day's classes. This information can also be obtained from a chart. Have the children place marks on their sundial bases each hour using a clock as a guide. Have them check it the next day to see how closely the shadow of the gnomon coincides with the correct hour. If the actual time and shadows are fairly close they have done a good job.

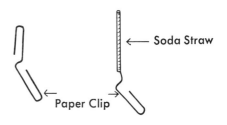

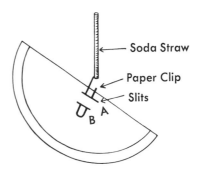

Note: Still another variation might be to use a piece of cardboard, lump of clay, and a pipe cleaner.

# SHAPES AND STRUCTURES

### How to Begin

Each child should receive a quarter pound of clay and discussion should immediately center around things they can make. Name some common objects such as blocks, houses, balls, people, animals, etc., and permit play with the clay. Children will want to verbalize about their structures. Listen to their explanations and do not be too eager to interpret or comment about their individual expressions. This beginning could be labeled "aimless play" with the clay. Your initial and immediate goal is to have brief contact with every child in the class in order to hear expressions about the objects each has selected to create.

Clay becomes the vehicle through which the teacher motivates free expression: the use of words, oftentimes very descriptive phrases, result Remember to be a good listener with each child.

### Why Do It This Way?

This activity presents the opportunity to deal with three-dimensional objects, or, as children sometimes say, "to make things that look like something." Why is reality important? The child's first descriptive words and phrases are about reality—how things look, feel, smell, or taste. Use real things as models for making clay objects. Let's find out what little fingers fashion from the observations of active minds. Do the descriptive words "fit" the real object, the created clay object, or any object? Is it always important for the descriptions to fit? Certainly much concern will initially be focused on how the clay feels: how it warms up, the handprints that can be made in it, the funny way it breaks.

Is it so bad to use science as the vehicle to get primary children to use words? Any clay object created can be the focal point around which you encourage verbalization: What it is? Where did it come from? How big is it in real life? Does it move? Is it living?

One important objective in this activity is to help develop a sense of shape, dimension, and structure. The initial pattern of free play during which clay objects are created can easily be directed toward particular shapes. This direction should come slowly. Gradually you will direct attention to particular shapes, sizes, and structures. Vocabulary unique to particular shapes can be developed.

### How to Do It

The various activities suggested for this unit are arbitrarily divided into lessons, but this does not imply that each lesson is one class period. A single lesson can require many class periods. It is important, however, to follow the progression of the lessons. A class lesson should be approximately thirty minutes.

#### Lesson 1

Give each youngster a quarter of a pound of clay. Permit time for play with the clay. Children should be encouraged to bring small boxes to school as storage containers for their clay.

Draw on the chalkboard a picture of a sphere, in three-dimensional perspective if you can, or, otherwise, merely draw a circle. Ask the children to make with their clay a model of what you have drawn. Tell the children what they have made is a *sphere.* Encourage the use of the word. Print it on the board. Let it become the word your class always uses instead of the word "ball." Talk about the sphere. Start developing a shapes-and-structure vocabulary. Keep a list on the board, or on a chart, throughout the unit.

#### Lesson 2

Have the children make another sphere. Speculate with them about what the sphere looks like on the inside: "How could we find out?" Let them work on that for a while. You may suggest, "What would a sphere look like if we cut it in half?" Cut the sphere in half, using a metal ruler.

Lead the children into discussions about the shape of the cut surface. It may be slightly out of shape, due to the cutting, but they will recognize it as a circle.

#### Lesson 3

Start with a sphere of clay once more. Have one child cut his sphere in half. Measure the diameter of the circle. Ask the children to guess: "If we make a sphere of one of the halves and cut it in two, will the diameter of the cut surface be ex-

actly half the original diameter of the larger sphere?" After they have made their guesses, perform the experiment. The word "diameter" may be new to the children. Take time in this lesson to decide how to make a diameter measurement. Construction paper strips can serve as rulers.

#### Lesson 4

Draw a cube on the board. Follow the same general steps for studying the cube as you used for the sphere. Try cutting the cube at various points. Discuss the resulting shapes.

## Lesson 5

Draw a cylinder on the board. Follow the same procedures, using it as the basic shape. Be sure the children cut the cylinder straight across and at two or three angles, to discover the ovals. Encourage discussion of these shapes. Ask, "Can anyone cut a cylinder in two and make a square surface?" Take as many class periods as necessary to let the children discover the many different shapes that result from cutting the cylinder.

## Lesson 6

Ask the children to make a thick cylinder and stand it on end. Then, ask them to roll it between their hands, asking, "What is happening to the cylinder?" Use words like "diameter" in normal classroom discussion, for children like to practice their new vocabulary. When the children have discovered that the cylinder gets smaller around and taller, ask, "How tall do you think it can get before it falls over?"

Do this experiment. Find out who can make the tallest cylinder. Ask the children why the cylinder falls over or collapses. Gradually, help them, through discussions, to realize that a shape or a structure must be strong enough to support its own weight.

## Lesson 7

The objective in this lesson is to make an arch out of a cylinder. Draw an arch on the board. Ask, "Who can make a structure like this with his clay?" Let them experiment before you supply any guidance. Ask the children to experiment with long cylinders standing on end and then standing as an arch. They will probably overextend the ability of the clay arch to stand. Discuss the relative height of a column and the length of cylinder that can be erected in the form of an arch.

Make measurements of diameters and lengths. Keep records. Here again is an opportunity to devise simple measuring schemes with construction paper strips.

## Lesson 8

Ask the children to roll out long cylinders. Ask part of the class to stand their cylinders on end, and elongate them up to the toppling point (compression).

The other part of the class will use the cylinders differently. Ask them to hold them up, suspended by one end. Tell the children to observe how thin the cylinders can be made and still be strong enough to hold together. Compare tension with compression. Is clay stronger in compression or in tension? The words "compression" and "tension" will be new and need explanation.

"Shapes and structures" can be fashioned from plastic soda straws and pipe cleaners. Each child should receive an assortment of soda straw lengths (one, two, three, and four inches) and about a dozen pipe cleaners (cut to four-inch lengths). The pipe cleaners are inserted into the straws and serve as "links" in joining straws together. For best results, the four-inch pipe cleaners should be doubled in half and each end bent about one half inch. This method insures a snug fit in the straws. Insert the "doubled end" in one end of a straw leaving the two "bent ends" available to receive one straw each. Successively connecting straws together in this manner will permit building of many two- and three-dimensional shapes.

Show the children how to make a cube so they gain confidence in the use of these new materials. After they see how to make a "cube soda straw structure" permit time for making various other structures. The structures can be named. Children can "join forces" and develop larger structures. Strength relationships will again become apparent. With your guidance the class may decide that some structural shapes are stronger than others.

This unit can be carried on almost indefinitely, working with relative strengths of shapes under compression or tension. Many clay and soda straw shapes can be considered. Other materials should be considered—such as plaster of paris, papier-mâché, etc.

# SINK OR FLOAT?

### How to Begin

This is a brief unit designed for primary youngsters. It deals with some very interesting relationships involving weight, volume, and density. The effect of buoyancy on different kinds of objects is investigated in this activity by the first-hand use of very simple materials. The children should be allowed to uncover some of the fundamental concepts concerning the phenomenon of buoyancy, as well as the identity of the objects with which they are working. Choosing partners for the experiments will add to the interest of the group by generating more active participation. Children should enjoy matching wits against each other as they make predictions and share ideas.

### Why Do It This Way?

Primary children love to explore their environment through the active use of their senses and by genuine participation. They have ample opportunity to do both in this activity. Young chil-

dren also tend to draw hasty conclusions as to whether an object will sink or float, for they generally have relatively little background experience to draw from. Complex questions involving such phenomena as the displacement of water and surface tension are not necessary at this level unless these questions are brought up by the children themselves.

The materials listed in this unit are for the convenience of the teacher. Other materials may be substituted if they are more readily available. Objects with distinct, bright colors were chosen to facilitate the association of the particular object with something readily observable by the child.

**How to Do It**

*Lesson 1*

Materials needed:

Plastic transparent water cups
Water
Little relish paper cups (red)
Small piece of tar (black)
Wood toothpicks (blue)
Small pieces of sponge (yellow)
Small leaves (green)
Pieces of rubber balloons (orange)
Cork material (brown)
Chips of white soap (floating and nonfloating
    types)
Little pieces of pink paper
Chocolate coins wrapped in gold paper
Paper towels

Each child should receive the above materials with which to conduct and record his own investigations.

This lesson might begin by asking the students to discuss the objects they have received. Suggest that they fill their plastic containers about two-thirds full with water. Ask them to guess whether the blue object (toothpick) will float or sink if they place one in their container of water. Have them record their prediction on the record sheet before actually experimenting. Follow the same procedure for each of the other objects. If the exercise is conducted with partners, make sure that the partner has made a prediction also. Ask the class to write the word "floats" on the line next to the object they tried if it does so. If the object sinks, they should write the word "sinks" in the appropriate column. Other methods of recording may be used to denote sinking or floating (e.g., an arrow pointing up or one pointing down). Let the children devise some methods of their own.

### SINK OR FLOAT RECORD SHEET

Write the word FLOAT or SINK in the correct column.

|  | Your Guess | Your Partner's Guess | What Actually Happened | Real Name of Object |
|---|---|---|---|---|
| Blue object |  |  |  |  |
| Yellow object |  |  |  |  |
| Red object |  |  |  |  |
| Brown object |  |  |  |  |
| Green object |  |  |  |  |
| White object |  |  |  |  |
| Pink object |  |  |  |  |
| Gold object |  |  |  |  |

### Lesson 2

An interesting variation involving a somewhat more sophisticated selection of materials can be tried if sufficient interest and enthusiasm have been generated.

The teacher should prepare one glass tumbler two-thirds full of water. A second tumbler should be two-thirds filled with alcohol. Place the two tumblers side by side on a table. Place some ice cubes in a tray next to the glasses. Ask the children to write down what they see. After sufficient time has been allowed to write down their observations, drop an ice cube into each of the tumblers and ask the students for reactions. There should be some confusion for the class is not aware that the glasses hold two different liquids.

123

(The ice will sink in the alcohol but will float in the water.) The class may appreciate the necessity for not jumping to hasty conclusions after this demonstration.

*Lesson 3*

The preceding two lessons should not be given on two consecutive days. Enough time should be permitted to allow the students to "digest" the results of their investigation. In addition, a time spread will offer the opportunity for the class to observe similar phenomena in their natural environment. A good deal of fascinating discussion can be had as a follow-up to the previous lessons, stimulated by such questions as "How do some insects float on water?" "Why do some people float easily and others do not?" "How can heavy objects like metals float?" "Do liquids other than water cause objects to float more easily?"

# THICKNESS OF FLUIDS

The primary child has had many experiences with paints, making mud pies, or splashing water. These are all gross experiences. No particular direction has been supplied which might focus attention more closely on particular characteristics. This unit will deal with a few measurable characteristics of fluids.

### How to Begin

Necessary materials should first be assembled in sufficient quantity:

test tubes (one per student)
shot #4
beebees
milk cartons (about 42)
paper cups (for beebees or shot)

newspapers and paper towels
#7 cork stoppers (4 dozen)
honey
automotive oil (#30 and #40)
cooking oil
syrup
corn syrup

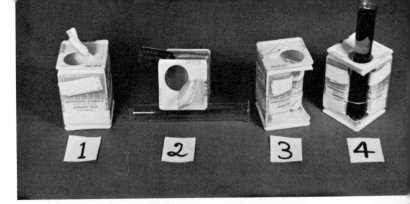

## Why Do It This Way?

Children have had many experiences with water—a fluid. They have not labeled water a fluid; in fact, this word is probably not a working part of their present vocabulary. They know water can be cool or hot. They have seen or made bubbles in water. Some things float in water, others sink. Not all water is clean. There are many other activities and characteristics which they associate with water or any fluid. This unit will concentrate on a characteristic associated with all fluids and through "doing activities" encourage children to form early concepts about the "flow of fluids."

## How to Do It

### Lesson 1

Start this unit by initiating a general discussion about water. What do the children know about water? Most of the responses will deal with how water is used or what it does rather than describe its physical characteristics (properties). In the discussion direct attention to other fluids: milk, soda, gasoline, syrup, etc. In what ways are these fluids similar? In what ways are they different? Consideration should be given to such things as color, smell, taste, and feel (some fluids have dangerous properties).

A word description chart can be developed. The term "fluid" should be used, not defined, and associated with characteristics similar to those of water.

### Lesson 2

Interesting activities will result from watching a bubble move in a fluid.

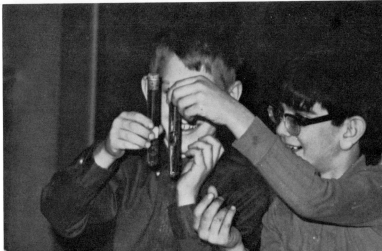

125

Fill ten test tubes with honey, ten with corn syrup (light Karo), and ten with water. Each test tube should be filled up to within one inch of the top. Place a #7 cork stopper securely in each test tube. Additional test tubes can be used,

either for new substances or for ones already suggested.

Supply each pair of youngsters with two test tubes (placed in milk cartons which act as holders). Suggest that the children watch the bubble move in their test tubes as they turn them upside down. Demonstrate for the children. This will start the activity. The teacher then can circulate in the room, listening to responses and suggesting certain observations.

There are many interesting observations. Bubbles move at different speeds in different fluids. Different-size bubbles in the same fluid move at different speeds. Children can time how long it takes for bubbles to move from one end of the test tube to the other end. Comparisons or "races" will cause happy excitement. Large bubbles elongate and their movement is affected by the sides of the test tube. Smaller bubbles are more spherical in shape and are not affected by the sides of the test tube. The tops of the bubbles look "silvery" because of the reflection of the light from above. Things look distorted when you look through the bubbles. Bubbles move very rapidly in water and appear to dance as they move up and down the tube. The test tube can be held horizontally—with the bubble in the center similar to a carpenter's level—and then rotated quickly by your fingers. The bubble does funny things: it "squeezes" together.

There are numerous things which can be done with bubbles trapped in a fluid. Use your imagination and permit time for the collection of information. "Thick" fluids (honey, Karo) allow closer observation because the bubbles move so slowly.

Move about the room listening to and encouraging individual responses and, when appropriate, have children exchange fluids. As previously noted, the most exciting fluids to examine are honey and clear corn syrup (Karo).

### Lesson 3

The initial encounter with fluids permitted time for "aimless play" and an accumulation of raw experience with various fluids. Now a new activity can be added. Give each child enough beebees

126

to place three in each test tube. The children will now observe not only the movement of the bubbles but also that of the beebees. Are the beebees affected by the bubbles in their movement? How does the size of a beebee appear to change as it goes past a bubble and on into the rest of the fluid? Does the beebee seem to move faster as it moves past a bubble? In which fluid do the beebees move fastest? In which one slowest? Can the "time of fall" for beebees be determined? A metronome will allow the children to count the "ticks" for "time of fall." Data can be assembled and bar graphs constructed.

Note that the bubbles can be completely eliminated by filling the test tubes all the way to the top, eliminating the air space below the cork.

As a demonstration the teacher can arrange test tubes filled with various fluids in a place clearly visible to all children and drop beebees into each test tube one at a time. Can the children arrange the fluids in order—fastest first and slowest last? Dropping beebees one at a time into the test tubes does not have to be a class demonstration. It can be performed by each pair of children. Each team will have to be supplied with more beebees than originally made available.

This activity of comparing "times to drop in a fluid" requires that children establish a procedure for making this comparison. Several are possible; for example, the "second" hand on a clock or a metronome. With the small test tubes children will find either of these procedures difficult for some fluids. One feature that can help make the demonstration-discussion successful is long containers in which to observe the shot fall through the fluid. One-half-inch diameter glass tubing cut in twelve- or sixteen-inch lengths and carefully stoppered at one end will work nicely. The longer tubes will amplify the differences in time for beebees to fall, especially in the liquids where the differences were only slight.

Based on their experiences with various fluids, children will conclude that some are not as "heavy," "sticky," "runny," or "thick" as others, and thus one characteristic of fluids, that they *flow* to varying degrees, has been identified.

All observations to this point have been with beebees or shot, but other objects, such as vari-

ous-size marbles and metal washers, can be used. It will be observed that the shape and size of the falling object affects the time of fall. How does size and/or shape affect dropping time? This can be checked by using various-size marbles or washers. Most objects will move smoothly through the liquid. Some objects may appear to vibrate or "chatter" as they fall through the liquid. Certain objects will create turbulences in the liquid which will cause this erratic motion.

This unit encourages the process of science. A skillful teacher can use it to develop techniques of observation, collection of information, and meaningful verbal as well as written descriptions of all the experiences. The primary youngster should have confrontations that permit him to practice these skills.

## TOPOLOGY FOR TOTS

### How to Begin

Do we see things as they really are? Here is an interesting activity for primary students involving very simple materials.

This unit may take one, two, or several days, depending upon the depth to which the teacher wishes to explore. The basic materials required are scissors, adding machine tape, scotch tape, and crayons.

### Why Do It This Way?

Children will have a good deal of fun in trying this activity. They will have an opportunity to make observations and then perform experiments based upon these observations. They then practice making predictions as to the end results and will enjoy the surprise outcomes as they differ from their earlier guesses and conclusions.

There are many additional implications for an activity such as this. For, once all variables are not controlled (a very difficult thing even for trained

scientists), the end results can be radically changed. A realization of the limitations of some of our senses can also be appreciated from this experiment.

This unit can serve as an entree into the way-out world of topology, a branch of mathematical science which deals with geometric shapes and special relationships among figures and patterns.

"Some of the best mathematical minds of today are engaged in working with this strange world of fascinating and improbable shapes. It deals with a special kind of geometry concerned with the ways in which surfaces can be twisted, bent, pulled, stretched, or otherwise deformed from one shape into another. Sometimes topologists deal with surfaces that no one could construct; sometimes they conceive of forms that seem impossible—e.g., a surface with only one side. Their special world of pure mathematics ranges from seeming child's play to difficult abstractions that leave even the experts puzzled.

Topologists like to quote a parody of the poem "Hiawatha," about an Indian who made some mittens of furry skin:

> He, to get the warm inside
> Put the inside skin side outside
> And to get the cold side outside
> Put the warm side fur side inside

In his mitten-twisting, the Indian was in fact performing a topological maneuver."[12]

Our astronauts will also be faced with unusual topological problems as they attempt to navigate across oceans of space to the moon and planets without familiar reference points.

Young children have been known to grasp fundamentals of topology more readily than adults. Apparently, they have not had time to be confused by experiences and conditioned responses and are able to appreciate the fact that, topologically speaking, a triangle and a circle are the same thing. If you doubt this, ask a young child to reproduce a picture of a triangle and you may

12 Reprinted from *Mathematics* by permission of Time-Life Books © 1963 Time Inc.

be surprised by how much it resembles a circle. When a child picks up a ball of modeling clay, squeezes it into the shape of a box, then flattens it into a dish, he is performing topological transformations in much the same way a scientist does as he explores the vagaries of geometric surfaces.

August Ferdinand Möbius (1790-1868) was a German astronomer and mathematician. He initiated many concepts concerning geometry that are recognized as standards today, and is especially well-known for his work in the field of topology. Möbius is probably best known for the invention of the one-sided surface that children are encouraged to make in this unit. It is often referred to as a Möbius band or strip.

## How to Do It

As a start, the teacher might introduce this unit by asking the class to watch carefully. Begin by holding a long pencil loosely between your thumb and index finger. Hold your arm upright and, keeping the forearm fairly rigid, while gripping the pencil lightly, rapidly move your whole arm up and down. An illusion is produced in which the pencil appears to be bending and flexing as though it were made of rubber. Let each child try it for himself. Once they are all in the spirit of things, ask them if they know any other tricks to make things appear different from what they really are. Initial activities of this kind are a good way to generate interest and will promote a questioning attitude in preparation for a lesson in topology.

Give each youngster a piece of paper about two inches wide and approximately twenty-four inches in length. (Adding machine tape or wrapping paper will do nicely.) How many sides does the paper have? How many edges does it have? Ask each youngster to write his first name on one side of the piece of paper and his last name on the reverse side. They can do this readily and the names will be an aid in identifying each side. It will be a somewhat different situation after they have put a half twist in their strips and try to color each side differently. Now ask each youngster to hold one end of the strip of paper in one hand and with his free hand give the paper a half twist. (The teacher may have to demonstrate first, and then help individuals who have some difficulty.)

Now have the child bring the two ends together and fasten them with paste or transparent tape. When each child has accomplished this he will have a Möbius strip, also called a Möbius band. Write the word "Möbius" on the board and help the class to pronounce it (moe · bias). Does the Möbius strip have any unusual properties? Try some of the following experiments with your pupils and see.

Have each student grasp the strip of twisted paper between his thumb and index finger and move his fingers along the entire length of paper. Ask the question, "Do you return to the same starting point?"

Ask the children how many sides their pieces of paper have now. Most will respond with the answer "two." Challenge them to color one side red and the other side blue with crayon. They will be quite surprised when the task proves impossible. Go one step further and ask how many edges the piece of paper has. Instruct them to hold the paper in one hand and trace one edge with the index finger of the other hand. By now they will be thoroughly perplexed and ask many questions.

Don't be too concerned over their bewilderment, for, remember, a laboratory is a place where questions are not always answered but where new questions are often shaped.

As an option for those children who wish to explore further, issue some scissors and ask the students to try cutting their Möbius strip down the center, but before doing so have them guess what the results will be. Again, there should be a great deal of surprise. Try it yourself. Still other variations can be attempted by cutting one-third of the way from the edge and continuing all around. The result of this cut will be even more startling than the first.

Another interesting activity that can be introduced to integrate language arts with science is to have youngsters try composing brief limericks about their Möbius strips similar to the one about Hiawatha. For example:

A mathematician confided
That a Möbius band is one-sided
And you'll get quite a laugh
If you cut one in half
For it stays in one piece when divided.

Many unusual and imaginative limericks will be generated by the children once they get the knack of it. Remember, in a limerick there must be five lines; lines 1, 2, and 5 should rhyme, as should 3 and 4.

# VIBRATING OBJECTS

The source of every sound is a vibrating object. From the rattle of a drum to the roar of a cannon, matter is set in motion and the energy of this motion is transmitted through some medium, either solid, liquid or gas. Other molecules are in turn vibrated and transmit these vibrations to our ears, where they are perceived and interpreted as particular sounds. We rely upon our sense of hearing constantly in daily existence. Even during sleep the ear mechanism continues to function and the brain to react, but on an unconscious level. We tend to take our delicate sense of hearing for granted and often do not appreciate the degree to which we are able to discriminate among different sounds. The human ear is much more sensitive to different frequencies of sound than is the eye to variations in color.

## How to Begin

Young children enjoy making sounds as well as listening to them. The following lessons involve students in both of these activities and utilize simple materials. Gather enough materials for each student individually to explore and investigate some of the phenomena of sound. A study of sound can include many activities. Experiments might range from the construction of simple sound-producing instruments such as a series of rubber bands of different thickness stretched across a wooden base to the playing of rhythm toys and conventional musical instruments.

One objective of this unit is to get primary children involved in a few investigations centered around the basic phenomena of sound. These include different media through which sound can travel, pitch, loudness, and frequency. The teacher is encouraged to let his imagination roam and to try new avenues for the exploration of sound based upon his own experience and the interest generated by the children. Let the following lessons serve as guide rather than a definitive approach to understanding sound.

Materials needed are straight pins, nails, rubber bands, tuning forks of different frequencies, string, an assortment of simple musical instruments—as many types as possible—rubber balloons, rice, pith balls, and cigar boxes.

## Why Do It This Way?

The science of sound can be investigated from two perspectives. In a pure physical sense, sound is produced by matter being set into motion. Thus, a sound is made any time an object is vibrated. If a sound is not heard by any human ear, is there a sound? The frequently posed riddle of whether there is a sound if a tree falls a thousand miles from any human ear involves a definition of terms. The perception of sound by a human ear is a physiological and biological phenomenon, but the subsequent interpretation by an intelligent brain is a subjective response and can be considered independently of the pure physics of sound. Therefore, to adequately discuss and investigate sound we must decide which definition we are going to use.

The normal range of hearing in humans is from about 16 vibrations per second to 20,000 VPS. Sounds exist below and far above this range, and many animals, such as bats, are capable of perceiving sounds far above 20,000 VPS. All of us,

children included, take our sense of hearing for granted, and few people appreciate the extreme sensitivity of the human ear.

In the following lessons students have the opportunity to investigate the delicacy of their sense of hearing and to explore some of the basic phenomena of sound.

## How to Do It

### Lesson 1

To begin this unit the teacher might ask the class to be absolutely quiet and listen and identify any sound they hear. They might make individual lists of these sounds, competing to see who can form the longest list. Children will become

aware of such sounds as the buzzing of the wall clock, the wind outside the window, someone walking down the hall, or even their own breathing, which had previously gone unnoticed.

Suggest that they now place their ears to their desks and listen intently for one minute. Urge them to record the sounds they hear. Ask questions such as: Do you hear any new sounds? Are they louder or softer? Are there more sounds

than when you listened without putting your ear to the desk? Many questions will arise from this experiment. How do other animals hear? Do insects hear sound? Do they have ears like people? Why are your ears important? What shape are they? Does the shape help you to hear better?

### Lesson 2

This activity is extremely simple and requires no materials other than the students' hands and the teacher's voice.

Begin this lesson by referring to previous questions concerning the shape of the ear. Ask students if they know the "scientific name" for the outer ear. (It's called the pinna. In many animals the pinna is larger than in humans and is movable.) Ask the class if anyone can move or wriggle his ears. They will delight in trying and in almost every class at least a few individuals will be capable of some pronounced movement. Ask what would happen if their ears were quite large and could be moved freely.

Suggest they try the following simple experiment. The teacher recites a few lines of a poem at a normal speaking voice level, and then asks the class to react to the general loudness. Now have each child cup his hands behind his ears (in effect, enlarging the area of the pinna). Then recite the same poem. Again ask the class to react in terms of any difference in loudness. The difference should be startling. Try cupping your hands to your lips (megaphone style) and try the experiment again.

An interesting variation is to have each child reverse the position of his hands so that the sound is captured from the rear. The teacher now repeats the poem and, by cupping his hands to his lips, bounces his voice off the rear wall to the students' ears. From this experiment a discussion of echoes can be initiated and children might relate experiences they have had with this phenomenon.

### Lesson 3

Spoken language depends entirely upon the ability of human beings to hear and monitor sounds. A young child acquires auditory skills by associating the sounds he hears with related experiences. There is tremendous variety in the sounds around us, and young children need guidance in learning to become aware of the different qualities and characteristics of sounds. Such characteristics as intensity, pitch, and timbre are often little understood. The following exercises are simple investigations in these areas. Just as the definition of sound can be explored from two perspectives, subjective and objective, individual characteristics can be investigated in a similar manner: for example, loudness is subjective and depends upon who is doing the hearing. "Intensity" is the result of the intrinsic energy of the sound and the distance one is from the source and the energy of the source. To demonstrate this phenomenon and to get youngsters involved in developing an understanding of loudness and intensity (for our purposes we use these words interchangeably) set up a tape recorder and microphone. Place the monitor switch in the rear of the tape recorder on "public address." If this feature is not available on your recorder, record the sounds produced for playback later. Ask a member of the class to stand one foot from the microphone and speak into it. Then have the student move progressively farther from the microphone at measured intervals of two, three, four, five feet, and so on. The children will be quite surprised at how rapidly the loudness of the sound falls off. (This is an example of the inverse square law.) As the child moves from one foot to two feet away from the mike the sound intensity does not drop off to one half the original intensity; rather, it diminishes by the inverse square—at two feet to 1/4, at three feet to 1/9, and at four feet to 1/16. Observe that at ten feet the sound intensity has dropped to 1/100 of the original sound. If a tape recorder is not available, the same principle can be investigated by having a child hold a portable radio at a preset volume and move through the various intervals. Do not attempt to go into great detail or specifics with youngsters of this age. Rather, allow them to glean a sense of appreciation for this phenomenon by being directly involved.

## Lesson 4

Materials: Drum, drumstick, pebbles, ball, fifteen tuning forks, a pan of water, comb, and tissue paper. The following is a list of brief but stimulating activities young children can try individually or in small groups. (Home-made drums of tin cans and balloons can be constructed by the students—see end of this unit for description.)

A. Have one student tap a small drum with a drumstick and ask other students to feel the top of the drum. In this way the children can both hear and "feel" the sound.

B. Place some sand or pebbles on the drum skin (scraps of paper or rice also should work well).

Children will enjoy seeing this material jump up and down as the energy of the vibrating drum skin is transmitted to objects placed upon it.

C. Divide the class into pairs of children. Give a tuning fork to each pair. Ask them to strike the tuning forks on their heels. (Caution them not to tap the forks on hard or sharp surfaces because they damage easily.) Then ask the youngsters to touch their tuning forks to a pan or tray of water and observe their reactions. (Lay newspapers on the desk tops to absorb spillage.)

Have the youngsters listen to the tuning forks. Ask them to try rotating the forks close to their ears. Their reaction should be interesting. (Rapidly rotating a vibrating tuning fork will produce a beating effect.)

D. Give each pair of children a tuning fork and pith ball (small spheres made from plants and attached to threads). If pith balls cannot be obtained, try small balls of aluminum foil. This is an extremely exciting activity and an excellent method of illustrating that sound is produced by something moving or vibrating. It is also a good way of dramatically aiding youngsters to understand that air can be made to vibrate.

Have one member of each team strike the tuning fork while the other tries to pass the pith ball down between the center of the tines. This will prove to be impossible as long as the tuning fork is vibrating strongly. The pith ball will be flung away from the center of the fork much to the astonishment and glee of the children.

E. Give each pair of students one cigar box and an assortment of rubber bands of various thicknesses. Have them slip a few of the bands around their cigar boxes. Plucking the elastic bands will produce a clearly audible sound. The box will act as a resonating device. Ask the class what kind of sound their elastic bands make. Does the thick rubber band make a high or a low sound? Does one band move (vibrate) faster than the other? Some children may be able to deduce the relationship between the number of times the elastic vibrates (frequency, an objective observation) with the pitch (a subjective observation) of the sound.

An interesting variation may be attempted by using a piece of string threaded through a hole in one end of a cigar box and over the other end and tied to a button. Different tones can be produced by pulling the button end of the string taut. If nylon thread or fishing line is used, simple tunes can be played with a little bit of practice.

F. Give each team an inexpensive comb and some tissue paper. Allow them to experiment freely. By plucking the teeth of the comb different sounds can be produced. Suggest that they

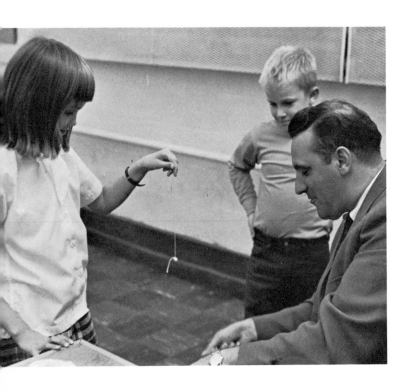

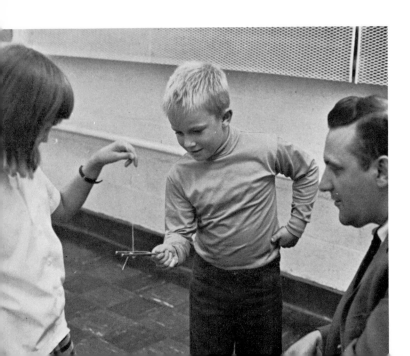

wrap the tissue over the comb and hold it lightly against their lips. Ask them to hum through this device and discuss what they feel and hear.

G. Suggest that one child place his finger lightly on his partner's throat in the area of the "adam's apple" while the other talks or sings. Ask them to describe what they feel. What produces the sound? Do some sounds "feel" different from others?

H. Ask the class to bring musical toys from home and have each child demonstrate his while the others try to guess what is causing the sound.

### Lesson 5

To demonstrate that sound can travel better through some materials than others try the following activities:

A. Fill an aquarium or large jar with water. Have students press their ears to the glass at each end. Lightly tap two rocks together in the water. Repeat the same experiment outside the container. Ask if there is any difference in the loudness of the sound produced.

B. Let one child hold a long wooden dowel or broomstick near his ear and press the other end against a ticking alarm clock. Can the sound be heard? Is it softer or louder?

C. Have each team make the "traditional" cup and string "telephone." Ask them to experiment with the string taut and slack. Try different cups: metal cans or paper. Use fishing line, waxed and unwaxed string. Let the children experiment on their own with variations of the "telephone,"

D. Have one student tie a string to the middle of the handle of a tuning fork and wrap one end of the string around each index finger and then put his fingers gently into his ears. Ask his teammate to tap the tines of the fork with a pencil. Have them reverse their roles and repeat the experiment.

### Lesson 6  Differences in Sound

A. Divide the class into groups of three or four and give each group a set of five or six soda bottles. Challenge them to produce a sound by blowing across the top. Suggest that they use water in the bottles at different levels and try making a sound again by blowing across the tops. Does the level of water in the bottle affect the sound?

B. Give each child a soft block of wood or a thick piece of cardboard and eight or ten small finishing nails or straight pins. Suggest that they push the pins into the wood or cardboard to different heights. By striking or plucking the pins and nails sounds can be produced. What kind of sounds are made by the longest pins? The shortest? Are the sounds different or the same?

C. Have each student try pulling a piece of stiff cardboard across the teeth of a pocket comb. Do it slowly at first. Then try it rapidly. Is there a difference in the sound produced? Does the pitch change? Does it get higher or lower?

D. Have one student press a ruler firmly at one end to a desk or table. Ask his partner to pluck the free end. Is a sound produced?

Does varying the length of the free end of the ruler cause differences in the pitch of the sound? Let the children experiment with different lengths and with varying amounts of force applied to the ruler (changes in pitch and amplitude should be observed).

E. An interesting variation of the rubber band and cigar box activity can be tried with a metal pie plate. Stretch a few rubber bands of different thicknesses around an empty pie plate and have the children pluck the bands. The metal plate will produce a resonance significantly different from that of the cigar box, and the class can also experiment with variations in pitch and amplitude.

F. If a piano, violin, guitar, or other stringed instrument is available, allow the children to examine it. How many observations can they make about the effect of thickness, tension, and length upon the kind of sound produced?

As an option have one of the children sing into a piano with the top open while another holds the loud pedal down. If all listen carefully they will hear the piano "sing" back as its strings vibrate sympathetically. A discussion of the effects of vibrations produced by large trucks on windowpanes in schools and houses may follow. Ask the children if they have had any related experiences.

In all the foregoing activities it might be wise to allow a few days between lessons to give the class time to observe similar phenomena in their environment.

Many of the references in the "Where to Find Out" section of this book offer additional ways in which students can use other vibrating objects and produce sounds for future exploration of acoustical phenomena.

In this unit just a few novel ways of performing simple experiments to investigate sound with primary children have been suggested as springboards. Try variations of your own.

Instructions for making individual toy drums: Collect empty coffee cans or equivalent-size containers. Give each student or group of students involved in making a drum a large piece of a rubber balloon and an elastic band. By stretching the piece of balloon over the open end of the can and securing it with the elastic a very satisfactory little drum can be made. Some coffee cans come with plastic covers for resealing and these can serve just as well. Pencils may be utilized as drumsticks.

# Where to Find Out

# WHERE TO FIND OUT

There are a tremendous number of science curriculum resources available to the elementary school teacher. National curriculum groups are currently producing generous quantities of material. Most of these materials emphasize student involvement and have as their central theme the process of science. Commercial publishers and equipment manufacturers have been greatly influenced by these national curriculum groups and are becoming more involved in the development of classroom materials to implement science programs.

Adoption of a science textbook series can no longer be considered sufficient to meet the needs of elementary school science. Textbook publishers realize this, and school systems are gradually coming to this decision. In fact, the multiple-text idea—coupled with a generous assortment of resource books (frequently paperback) and the material objects (supplies and equipment)—is becoming the common practice in classrooms.

The following material is resource material for the science units in this book. It should not be considered complete, for new and exciting material is constantly being produced.

**Reading and Visual Aid Material**

I. *Balancing Blocks*

A. Reading material for children

1. Darby, Gene, *What Is a Simple Machine?* (Benefic Press 1960)

2. Olschewski, Alfred, *Wheel Rolls Over* (Little, Brown 1962)

3. Pine, Tillie S. and Joseph Levine, *Friction All Around* (McGraw-Hill 1960)

4. Schneider, Herman and Nina, *Now Try This to Move a Heavy Load* (W. R. Scott 1947)

5. Sharp, Elizabeth N., *Simple Machines and How They Work* (Random House 1959)

6. Syrocki, B. John, *What Is a Machine?* (Benefic Press 1960)

B. Reading material for teachers

1. Bradley, Duane and Eugene Lord, *Here's How It Works* (Lippincott 1962)

2. Mann, Martin, *How Things Work* (Thomas Y. Crowell 1960)

3. Sootin, Harry, *Experiments With Machines and Matter* (Norton 1963)

C. Films

1. *Balancing Forces,* United World Films

2. *How Machines and Tools Help Us,* Coronet

3. *How Simple Machines Make Work Easier,* Coronet

4. *Machines,* Gateway

5. *Machines That Move Earth,* Film Associates of California

6. *You and Machines,* United World Films

7. *What's So Important About a Wheel?* Journal Films

D. Filmstrips

   1. *How Levers Help Us,* Filmstrip House

   2. *How Wedges Help Us,* Filmstrip House

   3. *Machines and Tools to Help Us Work,* Society for Visual Education

   4. *Wheels and Axles,* Jam Handy Organization

## II. *Bubbles*

A. Reading material for children

   1. Clymer, Eleanor, *Make Way for Water* (Messner 1953)

   2. McGrath, Thomas, *About Clouds* (Melmont 1959)

   3. Pine, Tillie S. and Joseph Levine, *Water All Around* (McGraw-Hill 1959)

   4. Podendorf, Illa, *True Book of Science Experiments* (Childrens Press 1954)

   5. Rukeyser, Muriel, *Bubbles* (Harcourt Brace & World 1967)

   6. Showers, Paul, *Find Out by Touching* (Thomas Y. Crowell 1961)

B. Reading material for teachers

   1. Boys, C. V., *Soap Bubbles and the Forces Which Mould Them* (Doubleday 1959)

   2. Bruce, G., *Experiments With Water* (National Science Teachers Association 1950)

   3. Ruchlis, Hy, *Bathtub Physics* (Harcourt Brace & World 1967)

## III. *Buttons, Beads, and "Things"*

A. Reading material for children

   1. Adler, Irving and Ruth, *Taste, Touch and Smell* (John Day 1966)

   2. Gottlieb, Suzanne, *What Is Red?* (Lothrop, Lee & Shepard 1961)

   3. Shapp, Charles and Martha, *Let's Find Out What's Light and What's Heavy* (Franklin Watts 1961)

   4. Showers, Paul, *Find Out by Touching* (Thomas Y. Crowell 1961)

   5. Vasiliu, Mircea, *The World Is Many Things* (John Day 1967)

B. Reading material for teachers

   1. Life Science Library: *Matter* (Time-Life Books 1965)

C. Films

   1. *Color,* Encyclopaedia Britannica

   2. *Form,* Encyclopaedia Britannica

   3. *Line,* Encyclopaedia Britannica

D. Filmstrips

   1. *Feel of Things,* Encyclopaedia Britannica

   2. *Smell of Things,* Encyclopaedia Britannica

   3. *Taste of Things,* Encyclopaedia Britannica

## IV. *Candle Making*

A. Reading material for teachers

   1. Adler, Irving, *Fire in Your Life* (John Day 1955)

   2. Bruce, G., *Fuels and Fire* (National Science Teachers Association 1951)

   3. Chemical Education Study: *Description of a Burning Candle* (W. H. Freeman 1963)

   4. Faraday, Michael, *Chemical History of a Candle* (Thomas Y. Crowell 1957)

B. Films

   1. *Fire: What Makes It Burn,* Encyclopaedia Britannica

   2. *Nature of Burning,* McGraw-Hill

C. Filmstrips

   1. *Some Things Dissolve,* McGraw-Hill

## V. *Changing Things*

A. Reading material for children

1. Carona, Philip B., *The True Book of Chemistry* (Childrens Press 1963)

2. Freeman, Mae and Ira, *The Story of Chemistry* (Random House 1962)

3. Hagman, Adaline P., *What Is Water?* (Benefic Press 1960)

4. Landin, Les, *Atoms for Junior* (Melmont 1961)

5. Lewellen, John, *The Mighty Atom* (Knopf 1955)

6. Straus, Jacqueline Harris, *Let's Experiment* (Harper & Row 1962)

7. Telfer, Dorothy, *About Salt* (Childrens Press 1965

8. Victor, Edward, *Molecules and Atoms* (Follett 1963)

B. Reading material for teachers

1. Adler, Irving and Ruth, *Atoms and Molecules* (John Day 1966)

2. Asimov, Isaac, *Building Blocks of the Universe* (Abelard-Schuman 1961)

3. Asimov, Isaac, *Inside the Atom* (Abelard-Schuman 1961)

4. Beeler, Nelson F. and Franklyn M. Branley, *Experiments in Chemistry* (Thomas Y. Crowell 1952)

5. Lessing, Lawrence P. *Understanding Chemistry* (New American Library 1959)

6. Milgrom, Harry, *Matter, Energy and Change: Exploration in Chemistry for Elementary School Children* (Manufacturing Chemists Association 1960)

7. Trieger, Seymour, *Atoms and Molecules* (Teachers Publishing Corporation 1964)

C. Films

1. *Chemical Changes All About Us,* Coronet

2. *Chemistry,* Gateway

3. *How Materials Are Alike and Different,* Coronet

4. *Simple Changes in Matter,* Coronet

5. *Solids, Liquids and Gases,* McGraw-Hill

6. *Things Dissolve,* McGraw-Hill

D. Filmstrips

1. *Finding Out How Things Change,* Society for Visual Education

2. *Important Chemical Elements,* Filmstrip House

VI. *Earthworms*

A. Reading material for children

1. Earle, Olive L., *Crickets* (William Morrow 1957)

2. Garelick, May, *Where Does the Butterfly Go When It Rains?* (W. R. Scott 1961)

3. Hogner, Dorothy C., *Grasshoppers and Crickets* (Thomas Y. Crowell 1960)

4. Hogner, Dorothy C., *Earthworms* (Thomas Y. Crowell 1953)

5. Kessler, Leonard, *The Worm, the Bird and You* (Dodd, Mead 1962)

6. Schoenknecht, Charles A., *Ants* (Follett 1960)

7. Selsam, Millicent E., *Terry and the Caterpillars* (Harper & Row 1962)

8. Sterling, Dorothy, *Caterpillars* (Doubleday 1961)

9. Stevens, Carla, *Catch a Cricket* (W. R. Scott 1961)

10. Zim, Herbert S., *What's Inside of Animals?* (William Morrow 1953)

B. Reading material for teachers

1. Barker, Will, *Familiar Animals of America* (Harper & Row 1956)

2. Wolfson, Albert and A. Ryan, *The Earthworm* (Harper & Row 1955)

C. Films

1. *How Animals Help Us,* Coronet

2. *Animals Move in Many Ways,* Film Associates of California

D. Filmstrips

   2. *Farmer's Animal Friends,* Jam Handy Organization

### VII. *Embryos*

A. Reading material for children

   1. Gans, Roma, *It's Nesting Time* (Thomas Y. Crowell 1964)

   2. Garelick, May, *What's Inside?* (W. R. Scott 1955)

   3. Hobson, Laura Z., *I'm Going to Have a Baby* (John Day 1967)

   4. King, Fred M. and George R. Otto, *What Is a Cell?* (Benefic Press 1961)

   5. Langstaff, N. and S. Szasz, *A Tiny Baby for You* (Harcourt Brace & World 1966)

   6. Podendorf, Illa, *The True Book of Animal Babies* (Childrens Press 1955)

   7. Schloat, G. Warren, *Wonderful Egg* (Scribner's 1952)

   8. Schwartz, Elizabeth and Charles, *When Animals Are Babies* (Holiday House 1964)

   9. Selsam, Millicent, *All About Eggs* (W. R. Scott 1952)

  10. Selsam, Millicent, *Egg to Chick* (International Publishers 1946)

  11. Ylla, and Arthur Gregor, *Animal Babies* (Harper & Row 1959)

B. Reading material for teachers

   1. Bosiger, E., and J. M. Guilcher, *A Bird Is Born* (Sterling 1959)

   2. Life Science Library: *Mammals* (Time-Life Books 1966)

C. Films

   1. *Baby Animals,* McGraw-Hill

   2. *Eggs to Chickens,* Bailey Films

   3. *Farm Animals,* Encyclopaedia Britannica

   4. *Mother Hen's Family,* Coronet

D. Filmstrips

   1. *Animal Babies,* Society for Visual Education

   2. *Animal Homes,* McGraw-Hill

   3. *How Animal Babies Grow,* Society for Visual Education

### VIII. *Fun with a Magnifying Glass*

A. Reading material for children

   1. Neurath, Marie, *Too Small to See* (Sterling 1957)

   2. Pine, Tillie S. and Joseph Levine, *Light All Around* (McGraw-Hill 1961)

B. Reading material for teachers

   1. Bragg, William, *The Universe of Light* (Dover 1940)

   2. Ruchlis, Hy, *The Wonder of Light* (Harper & Row 1960)

   3. Ruechardt, Eduard, *Light: Visible and Invisible* (University of Michigan Press 1958)

   4. Schwartz, Julius, *Through the Magnifying Glass* (McGraw-Hill 1954)

C. Films

   1. *All About Light,* Cenco Films

   2. *Animals See in Many Ways,* Film Association of California

   3. *Coco Takes His Magnifying Glass into the Garden,* Rampart Productions

   4. *Light and What It Does,* Encyclopaedia Britannica

   5. *Light for Beginners,* Coronet

   6. *Prove It With a Magnifying Glass,* Film Associates of California

D. Filmstrips

   1. *Light,* McGraw-Hill

   2. *The Story of Light,* McGraw-Hill

IX. *Guppies*

A. Reading material for children

1. Aliki, *My Five Senses* (Thomas Y. Crowell 1962)

2. Campbell, Elizabeth, *Fins and Tails* (Little, Brown 1963)

3. Darby, Gene, *What Is a Fish* (Benefic Press 1958)

4. Fenton, Carroll Lane, *Goldie Is a Fish* (John Day 1961)

5. Krauss, Ruth, *The Growing Story* (Harper & Row 1947)

6. Lionni, Leo, *Swimmy* (Pantheon 1963)

7. May, Charles Paul, *Box Turtle Lives in Armor* (Hale 1965)

8. McClung, Robert M., *Bufo: The Story of a Toad* (William Morrow 1954)

9. Miller, Patricia K. and Iran L. Seligman, *Big Frogs, Little Frogs* (Holt, Reinhart & Winston 1963)

10. Miller, Patricia K. and Iran L. Seligman, *You Can Find a Snail* (Holt, Reinhart & Winston 1963)

11. Neurath, Marie, *Growing* (Sterling 1963)

12. Selsam, Millicent, *Plenty of Fish* (Harper & Row 1960)

13. Ylla, and Arthur Gregor, *Animal Babies* (Harper & Row 1959)

14. Zim, Herbert S., *What's Inside of Me?* (William Morrow 1952)

B. Reading material for teachers

1. Life Science Library: *Ecology* (Time-Life Books 1963)

2. Herald, Earl, *Living Fishes of the World* (Doubleday 1961)

3. Jahn, Theodore L., *How to Know the Protozoa* (W. C. Brown 1949)

4. Life Nature Library: *The Fishes* (Time-Life Books 1965)

5. Morgan, Alfred P., *An Aquarium Book for Boys and Girls* (Scribner's 1959)

6. National Science Teachers Association, *How to Care for Living Things in the Classroom* (National Science Teachers Association 1965)

7. Prescott, Gerald W., *How to Know the Freshwater Algae* (W. C. Brown 1954)

C. Films

1. *Aquarium Wonderland,* Pat Dowling Pictures

2. *Living and Growing,* Churchill-Wexler Film Productions

3. *Pond Life,* Encyclopaedia Britannica

4. *Snails: Backyard Science,* Film Associates of California

5. *Story of a Frog,* United World Films

6. *We Get Food from Plants and Animals,* McGraw-Hill

D. Filmstrips

1. *Fish,* Curriculum Materials Corporation

2. *The Aquarium,* McGraw-Hill

3. *Toads Grow,* Jam Handy Organization

X. *Hot and Cold*

A. Reading material for children

1. Adler, Irving and Ruth, *Air* (John Day 1962)

2. Adler, Irving, *Fire in Your Life* (John Day 1955)

3. Parker, Bertha, *Thermometers, Heat and Cold* (Harper & Row 1959)

4. Schneider, Herman and Nina, *Let's Find Out: A Picture Science Book* (W. R. Scott 1946)

5. Schneider, Herman and Nina, *Let's Look Inside Your House* (W. R. Scott 1946)

B. Reading material for teachers

1. Adler, Irving, *Hot and Cold* (John Day 1959)

2. Ruchlis, Hy, *The Wonder of Heat Energy* (Harper & Row 1961)

3. Sootin, Harry, *Experiments With Heat* (Norton 1964)

C. Films

    1. *Air and What It Does,* Encyclopaedia Britannica

    2. *Heat-Molecules in Motion,* Charles Cahill

    3. *Understanding Fire,* Coronet

D. Filmstrips

    1. *Finding Out About Heating Solids Liquids and Gases,* Society for Visual Education

    2. *First Experiments With Heat,* Jam Handy Organization

    3. *How a Thermometer Works,* Filmstrip House

    4. *How Heat Helps Us,* Filmstrip House

    5. *How Heat Moves,* Filmstrip House

    6. *How Hot and How Cold,* McGraw-Hill

    7. *Where Heat Comes From,* Filmstrip House

## XI. *Magnets*

A. Reading material for children

    1. Adler, Irving and Ruth, *Magnets* (John Day 1966)

    2. Branley, Franklyn M. and Eleanor K. Vaughan, *Mickey's Magnet* (Thomas Y. Crowell 1956)

    3. Keen, Martin, *How and Why Wonder Book of Magnets and Magnetism* (Grosset & Dunlap 1963)

    4. Pine, Tillie S. and Joseph Levine, *Magnets and How to Use Them* (McGraw-Hill 1958)

    5. Podendorf, Illa, *True Book of Magnets and Electricity* (Childrens Press 1961)

    6. Reuben, Gabriel, *What Is a Magnet?* (Benefic Press 1959)

B. Reading material for teachers

    1. Lee, Eric, W., *Magnetism* (Penguin 1963)

    2. Parasnis, D. S., *Magnetism: From Lodestone to Polar Wandering* (Harper & Row 1962)

C. Films

    1. *Magnets,* McGraw-Hill

    2. *Michael Discovers the Magnet,* Encyclopaedia Britannica

    3. *The Story of Magnetism,* United World Films

D. Filmstrips

    1. *Different Kinds of Magnets,* Jam Handy Organization

    2. *Discovering Magnets,* Jam Handy Organization

    3. *Magnetism and Electricity,* Society for Visual Education

    4. *Magnets Help to Find Direction,* Jam Handy Organization

## XII. *Measurement for Wee People*

A. Reading material for children

    1. Adler, Irving, *Hot and Cold* (John Day 1959)

    2. Epstein, Sam and Beryl, *The First Book of Measurement* (Franklin Watts 1960)

    3. Kohn, Bernice, *Everything Has a Size* (Prentice-Hall 1964)

    4. Parker, Bertha M., *Thermometers, Heat and Cold* (Harper & Row 1959)

    5. Schneider, Herman and Nina, *How Big Is Big—From Stars to Atoms* (W. R. Scott 1946)

    6. Shapp, Charles and Martha, *Let's Find Out What's Light and What's Heavy* (Franklin Watts 1961)

B. Reading material for teachers

    1. Barker, Charles M., and others, *New Math for Teachers and Parents of Elementary School Children* (New American Library n.d.)

    2. *Manual for Measurement Science* (Ohaus Scale Corp 1965)

    3. Asimov, Isaac, *The Realm of Numbers* (Houghton Mifflin 1959)

    4. Gardner, Martin, *Relativity for the Million* (Macmillan 1962)

C. Films

    1. *Let's Measure Inches, Feet, and Yards,* Coronet

    2. *Let's Measure Ounces, Pounds, and Atoms,* Coronet

D. Filmstrips

    1. *Why Is the Night Cooler Than the Day?* Jam Handy Organization

### XIII. *Plants Without Sunlight*

A. Reading material for children

    1. Frahm, Anne, *True Book of Bacteria* (Children's Press 1963)

    2. Kavaler, Lucy, *Mushrooms, Molds, and Miracles; The Strange Realm of Fungi* (John Day 1965)

    3. Kavaler, Lucy, *The Wonders of Fungi* (John Day 1964)

    4. Lubell, Winifred and Cecil, *Green Is for Growing* (Rand McNally 1964)

B. Reading material for teachers

    1. Christensen, C. M., *The Molds and Man* (University of Minnesota Press 1965)

    2. Kohn, Bernice, *Our Tiny Servants: Molds and Yeasts* (Prentice-Hall 1962)

    3. Kreig, Margaret, *Green Medicine: The Search for Plants That Heal* (Rand McNally 1964)

C. Films

    1. *Living and Non-Living Things,* Coronet

    2. *What's Alive,* Film Associates of California

### XIV. *Planting Seeds*

A. Reading material for children

    1. Foster, Willene R. and P. Queree, *Seeds Are Wonderful* (Childrens Press 1960)

    2. Huntington, Harriet, *Let's Go to the Desert* (Doubleday 1949)

    3. Jordan, Helene J., *Seeds by Wind and Water* (Thomas Y. Crowell 1962)

    4. Podendorf, Illa, *The True Book of Plant Experiments* (Childrens Press 1960)

    5. Selsam, Millicent E., *Play With Plants* (William Morrow 1949)

    6. Webber, Irma, *Bits That Grow Big* (W. R. Scott 1949)

    7. Wood, Dorothy, *Plants With Seeds* (Follet 1962)

    8. Zim, Herbert S., *What's Inside of Plants* (William Morrow 1952)

B. Reading material for teachers

    1. Jensen, William A. and Leroy G. Kavaljian, *Plant Biology Today* (Wadsworth 1966)

    2. Corner, E. J. H., *The Life of Plants* (World Publishing 1964)

    3. Coulter, Merle Crowe, *The Story of the Plant Kingdom* (University of Chicago Press 1964)

C. Films

    1. *From Seeds to Plants,* Gateway

    2. *How Does a Garden Grow?,* Film Associates of California

    3. *Let's Watch Plants Grow,* Coronet

    4. *Seeds Grow Into Plants,* Coronet

D. Filmstrips

    1. *How Seeds Are Scattered,* Encyclopaedia Britannica

    2. *How Plants Live,* Encyclopaedia Britannica

    3. *How Seeds Sprout and Grow Into Plants,* Encyclopaedia Britannica

    4. *Plant Needs,* Encyclopaedia Britannica

### XV. *Rock Sorting*

A. Reading material for children

    1. Adler, Irving and Ruth, *The Earth's Crust* (John Day 1963)

2. Comfort, Iris Tracy, *Earth Treasures: Rocks and Minerals* (Prentice-Hall 1964)

3. Cormack, Maribelle B., *The First Book of Stones* (Franklin Watts 1950)

4. Darby, Gene, *What Is the Earth* (Benefic Press 1961)

5. Gans, Roma, *The Wonder of Stones* (Thomas Y. Crowell 1963)

6. Heavilin, Jay, *Beginning Knowledge Book of Rocks and Gems* (Macmillan 1964)

7. Podendorf, Illa, *The True Book of Pebbles and Shells* (Childrens Press 1954)

8. Podendorf, Illa, *The True Book of Rocks and Minerals* (Childrens Press 1958)

9. Shuttlesworth, Dorothy, *The Doubleday First Guide to Rocks* (Doubleday 1963)

10. Syrocki, John B., *What Is Soil?* (Benefic Press 1961)

B. Reading material for teachers

1. Beiser, Arthur and the Editors of Life, *The Earth* (Time-Life Books 1962)

2. Berckhemer, Fritz, *Language of Rocks* (Ungar 1957)

3. MacFall, Russell P., *Collecting Rocks, Minerals, Gems and Fossils* (Hawthorn 1964)

4. Pearl, Richard M., *Rocks and Minerals* (Barnes & Noble 1956)

5. Ransom, Jay Ellis, *Rock-hunter's Range Guide* (Harper & Row 1962)

C. Films

1. *Finding Out About Rocks,* United World Films

2. *Minerals and Rocks: Stones of The Earth,* Encyclopaedia Britannica

3. *Materials of Our Earth,* United World Films

4. *Our Earth,* Cenco Films

D. Filmstrips

1. *How the Earth's Surface Changes,* Filmstrip House

2. *Rocks and How They Change,* Filmstrip House

3. *Rocks and Minerals,* Society for Visual Education

XVI. *Shadows and Sundials*

A. Reading material for children

1. Adler, Irving and Ruth, *The Calendar* (John Day 1967)

2. Adler, Irving and Ruth, *Shadows* (John Day 1961)

3. Branley, Franklyn M., *North, South, East and West* (Thomas Y. Crowell 1966)

4. Branley, Franklyn M., *The Sun: Our Nearest Star* (Thomas Y. Crowell 1961)

5. Branley, Franklyn M., *What Makes Day and Night* (Thomas Y. Crowell 1961)

6. Bulla, Clyde R., *What Makes a Shadow?* (Thomas Y. Crowell 1962)

7. De Regniers, Beatrice S. and Isabell Gordon, *The Shadow Book* (Harcourt, Brace & World 1960)

8. Hamberger, John, *The Day the Sun Disappeared* (Norton 1964)

9. Jupo, Frank, *The Adventure of Light* (Prentice-Hall 1958)

10. Kettelkamp, Larry, *Shadows* (William Morrow 1957)

11. Schwartz, Julius, *Now I Know* (McGraw-Hill 1955)

B. Reading material for teachers

1. Life Science Library, *Time* (Time-Life Books 1966)

2. Ruchlis, Hy, *The Wonder of Light* (Harper & Row 1960)

C. Films

1. *Light and Shadow,* McGraw-Hill

2. *Light for Beginners,* Coronet

3. *Shadows,* NET Film Service

4. *Shadows on Our Turning Earth,* Film Associates of California

D. Filmstrips

   1. *Night and Day,* Encyclopaedia Britannica

   2. *Our Home—The Earth,* Society for Visual Education

## XVII. *Shapes and Structures*

A. Reading material for children

   1. Aliki, *My Five Senses* (Thomas Y. Crowell 1962)

   2. Kohn, Bernice, *Everything Has a Shape* (Prentice-Hall 1964)

B. Reading material for teachers

   1. Elementary Science Study *Teachers Guide-Attribute Games* (McGraw-Hill, Webster Division 1966)

   2. Elementary Science Study *Geo-Blocks* (McGraw-Hill, Webster Division 1967)

C. Films

   1. *Shapes,* Peter Hollander

## XVIII. *Sink or Float?*

A. Reading material for children

   1. Alexander, Anne, *Boats and Ships from A to Z* (Rand McNally 1961)

   2. Bendick, Jeanne, *Archimedes and the Door of Science* (Franklin Watts 1962)

   3. Gans, Roma, *Icebergs* (Thomas Y. Crowell 1964)

   4. Greenhood, David, *Watch the Tides* (Holiday House 1961

   5. Larrick, Nancy, *See for Yourself* (Dutton 1952)

   6. Marcus, Rebecca B., *Science in the Bathtub* (Franklin Watts 1961)

   7. Shapp, Charles and Martha, *Let's Find Out What's Light and What's Heavy* (Franklin Watts 1961)

B. Films

   1. *Boats and Ships,* Encyclopaedia Britannica

   2. *Water Pressure,* NET Film Service

   3. *Finding Out About the Water Cycle,* United World Films

C. Filmstrips

   1. *Air Helps Things to Float in Water,* Jam Handy Organization

   2. *Experiences With Water,* Eye Gate House

   3. *How Does Water Get into the Air?* Jam Handy Organization

   4. *Water, Water Everywhere,* McGraw-Hill

## XIX. *Thickness of Fluids*

A. Reading material for children

   1. Adler, Irving and Ruth, *Air* (John Day 1962)

   2. Ames, Gerald and Rose Wyler, *Prove It* (Harper & Row 1963)

   3. Hagaman, A., *What Is Water?* (Benefic Press 1961)

   4. Meyer, Jerome S., *Water at Work* (World Publishing 1963)

   5. Piltz, Albert, *What Is Air?* (Benefic Press 1960)

   6. Smith, F. C., *First Book of Water* (Franklin Watts 1959)

B. Reading material for teachers

   1. Life Science Library, *Water* (Time-Life Books 1967)

C. Films

   1. *Air and What It Does,* Encyclopaedia Britannica

   2. *How Air Helps Us,* Coronet

   3. *How Water Helps Us,* Coronet

   4. *Nothing But Air,* Encyclopaedia Britannica

5. *Water and What It Does,* Encyclopaedia Britannica

D. Filmstrips

1. *Finding Out About Heating Solids, Liquids, and Gases,* Society for Visual Education

2. *Finding Out About Land, Air, and Water,* Society for Visual Education

3. *How Does Water Get into the Air?,* Jam Handy Organization

### XX. *Topology for Tots*

A. Reading material for children

1. Kohn, Bernice, *Everything Has a Size* (Prentice-Hall 1964)

2. Showers, Paul, *Find Out by Touching* (Thomas Y. Crowell 1961)

B. Reading material for teachers

1. Arnold, B. H., *Intuitive Concepts in Elementary Topology* (Prentice-Hall 1962)

2. Elementary Science Study *Teachers Guide-Attribute Games* (McGraw-Hill, Webster Division 1966)

3. Life Science Library, *Mathematics* (Time-Life Books, 1963)

### XXI. *Vibrating Objects*

A. Reading material for children

1. Adler, Irving and Ruth, *Your Ears* (John Day 1963)

2. Anderson, Dorothy S., *Junior Science Book of Sound* (Garrard 1962)

3. Borten, Helen, *Do You Hear What I Hear?* (Abelard-Schuman 1960)

4. Knight, David C., *The First Book of Sound* (Franklin Watts 1960)

5. Meyer, Jerome S., *Sound and Its Reproduction* (World Publishing 1964)

6. Pine, Tillie S. and Joseph Levine, *Sounds All Around* (McGraw-Hill 1958)

7. Podendorf, Illa, *The True Book of Sounds We Hear* (Childrens Press 1955)

8. Showers, Paul, *How to Talk* (Thomas Y. Crowell 1966)

9. Showers, Paul, *The Listening Walk* (Thomas Y. Crowell 1961)

10. Tannenbaum, H. E. and Nathan Stillman, *We Read About Sounds and How They Are Made* (McGraw-Hill 1960)

B. Reading material for teachers

1. Blanc, Abraham, Gordner, *How Does the Body React?, Modern Science 2* (Holt, Rinehart & Winston 1963)

2. Fuller, Elizabeth M. and Mary J. Ellis, *Learning How to Use the Five Senses* (Denison 1961)

3. Moon, Truman J. and others, *Modern Biology* (Holt, Rinehart & Winston 1963)

C. Films

1. *Sounds All About Us,* Coronet

2. *Sound and How It Travels,* Encyclopaedia Britannica

3. *Sounds Around Us,* Cenco Films

4. *Sounds for Beginners,* Coronet

5. *What Is Sound?,* McGraw-Hill

D. Filmstrips

1. *Better to Hear You*, Encyclopaedia Britannica

2. *Finding Out About Sound,* Society for Visual Education

3. *Light, Heat and Sound,* Society for Visual Education

4. *Sounds We Hear,* Society for Visual Education

1. Elementary Science Study—Educational Development Center, Inc., 55 Chapel Street, Newton, Mass. 02160 (formerly Educational Services Inc.)

2. Science Curriculum Improvement Study, Department of Physics, University of California, Berkeley, Calif. 94720

3. AAAS Commission on Science Education, 1515 Massachusetts Avenue, N.W., Washington, D.C. 20005

4. Elementary School Science Project, Department of Botany, University of California, Berkeley, Calif. 94720

5. School Science Curriculum Project, College of Education, University of Illinois, Urbana, Ill. 61803

6. Quantitative Approach in Elementary School Science, Department of Physics, State University of New York, Stony Brook, N.Y. 11790

7. Elementary School Science Improvement Project, Department of Physics, Utah State University, Logan, Utah 84321

8. Minnesota Mathematics and Science Teaching Project, Minnesota School Mathematics and Science Center, University of Minnesota, Minneapolis, Minn. 55455

| Publisher | Address |
|---|---|
| Abelard-Schuman, Ltd. | 6 West 57 Street, New York, N.Y. 10019 |
| Abingdon Press | 201 Eighth Avenue South, Nashville, Tenn. 37202 |
| Addison-Wesley Publishing Co. | Reading, Mass. 01867 |
| Allyn and Bacon, Inc. | 470 Atlantic Avenue, Boston, Mass. 02110 |
| American Book Company | 55 Fifth Avenue, New York, N.Y. 10003 |
| American Education Publications | 55 High Street, Middletown, Conn. 06457 |
| American Library Association | 50 East Huron Street, Chicago, Ill. 60611 |
| American Technical Society | 848 East 58 Street, Chicago, Ill. 60637 |
| A. S. Barnes & Co. | Forsgate Drive, Cranbury, N.J. 08512 |
| Barnes and Noble Inc. | 105 Fifth Avenue, New York, N.Y. 10003 |
| Benefic Press | 10300 West Roosevelt Road, Westchester, Ill. 60153 |
| | 809 West Detweiller Drive, Peoria, Ill. 61614 |
| Chas. A. Bennett Company, Inc. | 7 East 51 Street, New York, N.Y. 10022 |
| Benziger Brothers Publishing Co. | 4300 West 62 Street, Indianapolis, Ind. 46206 |
| The Bobbs-Merrill Co. Inc. | 400 North Broadway, Milwaukee, Wis. 53201 |
| The Bruce Publishing Company | 850 Third Avenue, New York, N.Y. 10022 |
| Capitol Publishing Co., Inc. | 124 Spear Street, San Francisco, Calif. 94105 |
| Chandler Publishing Co. | |

| | |
|---|---|
| University of Chicago Press | 5750 Ellis Avenue, Chicago, Ill. 60637 |
| Childrens Press, Inc. | 1224 West Van Buren Street, Chicago, Ill. 60607 |
| Chilton Book Company | 401 Walnut Street, Philadelphia, Pa. 19106 |
| Coward-McCann, Inc. | 200 Madison Avenue, New York, N.Y. 10016 |
| Thomas Y. Crowell Company | 201 Park Avenue South, New York, N.Y. 10003 |
| Crown Publishers, Inc. | 419 Fourth Avenue, New York, N.Y. 10016 |
| T. S. Denison & Company, Inc. | 315 Fifth Avenue South, Minneapolis, Minn. 55415 |
| Dodd, Mead & Company | 79 Madison Avenue, New York, N.Y. 10016 |
| Doubleday and Company, Inc. | Garden City, N.Y. 11530 |
| Dover Publications | 180 Varik Street, New York, N.Y. 11530 |
| Earth Science Curriculum Project | Boulder, Colorado, 80301 |
| E. P. Dutton & Company, Inc. | 201 Park Avenue South, New York, N.Y. 10003 |
| Encyclopaedia Britannica, Inc. | 425 North Michigan Avenue, Chicago, Ill. 60611 |
| Feron Publishers, Inc. | 2165 Park Boulevard, Palo Alto, Calif. 94306 |
| The Fideler Company | 31 Ottawa Avenue N.W., Grand Rapids, Mich. 49502 |
| Follett Publishing Company | 1010 West Washington Boulevard, Chicago, Ill. 60607 |
| W. H. Freeman and Company | 660 Market Street, San Francisco, Calif. 94104 |
| Friendship Press | 475 Riverside Drive, New York, N.Y. 10027 |
| Garrard Publishing Co. | 1607 North Market Street, Champaign, Ill. 61820 |
| Ginn and Company | Statler Building Back Bay, P.O. 191, Boston, Mass. 02117 |
| Globe Book Company, Inc. | 175 Fifth Avenue, New York, N.Y. 10010 |
| Golden Press, Inc. (Education Division) | 850 Third Avenue, New York, N.Y. 10022 |
| Goodheart-Willcox Co. | 18250 Harwood Avenue, Homewood, Ill. 60430 |
| Grosett & Dunlap, Inc. | 51 Madison Avenue, New York, N.Y. 10010 |
| E M. Hale and Company | 1201 South Hastings Way, Eau Claire, Wis. 54701 |
| Harcourt, Brace & World, Inc. | 757 Third Avenue, New York, N.Y. 10017 |
| Harper and Row, Publishers, Inc. | 49 East 33 Street, New York, N.Y. 10016 |
| Hastings House Publishers, Inc. | 151 East 50 Street, New York, N.Y. 10022 |
| Hawthorn Books, Inc. | 70 Fifth Avenue, New York, N.Y. 10011 |
| D. C. Heath & Company | 285 Columbus Avenue, Boston, Mass 02116 |
| Hebrew Publishing Company, Inc. | 79 Delancey Street, New York, N.Y. 10002 |
| Holiday House Inc. | 18 East 56 Street, New York, N.Y. 10022 |
| Holt, Rinehart & Winston, Inc. | 383 Madison Avenue, New York, N.Y. 10017 |
| Houghton Mifflin Company | 2 Park Street, Boston, Mass. 02107 |

| | |
|---|---|
| International Text Book Co. | Scranton, Pa. 18515 |
| The John Day Company, Inc. | 62 West 45 Street, New York, N.Y. 10036 |
| Alfred A. Knopf, Inc. | 501 Madison Avenue, New York, N.Y. 10022 |
| Laidlaw Brothers | Thatcher & Madison Streets, River Forest, Ill. 60305 |
| J. B. Lippincott Company | East Washington Square, Philadelphia, Pa. 19105 |
| Little, Brown and Company | 34 Beacon Street, Boston, Mass. 02106 |
| Lothrop, Lee & Shepard Company, Inc. | 381 Park Avenue South, New York, N.Y. 10016 |
| Lyons & Carnahan | 407 East 25 Street, Chicago, Ill. 60616 |
| The Macmillan Company | 866 Third Avenue, New York, N.Y. 10022 |
| David McKay Company, Inc. | 750 Third Avenue, New York, N.Y. 10017 |
| Macrae Smith Co. | 225 South 15 Street, Philadelphia, Pa. 19102 |
| Manufacturing Chemists Association | 1825 Connecticut Avenue N.W., Washington, D.C. 20009 |
| McCormick-Mathers Publishing Company | P.O. Box 2212, 1440 East English Street, Wichita, Kans. 67201 |
| McGraw-Hill Book Company | 330 West 42 Street, New York, N.Y. 10036 |
| McNight & McNight Publishing Co. | Bloomington, Ill. 61701 |
| Melmont Publishers, Inc. | 1224 West Van Buren Street, Chicago, Ill. 60607 |
| Charles E. Merrill Books, Inc. | 1300 Alum Creek Dr., Columbus, Ohio 43216 |
| Julian Messner (Division of Simon & Schuster, Inc.) | 1 West 39 Street, New York, N.Y. 10018 |
| University of Michigan Press | Ann Arbor, Mich. 48106 |
| University of Minnesota Press | 2037 University Avenue S.E., Minneapolis, Minn. 55455 |
| William Morrow & Company, Inc. | 425 Park Avenue South, New York, N.Y. 10016 |
| National Science Teachers Association | 1201 16 Street, Washington, D.C. |
| Thomas Nelson & Sons | 1626 Copewood, Camden, N.J. 08103 |
| The New American Library Inc. | 1301 Avenue of the Americas, New York, N.Y. 10019 |
| New York Graphic Society, Ltd. | 104 Greenwich Avenue, Greenwich, Conn. 06830 |
| Noble and Noble Publishers, Inc. | 750 Third Avenue, New York, N.Y. 10017 |
| W. W. Norton & Company Inc. | 55 Fifth Avenue, New York, N.Y. 10003 |
| Pantheon Books | 22 East 51 Street, New York, N.Y. 10022 |
| Penguin Books Inc. | 7110 Ambassador Road, Baltimore, Md. 21207 |
| J. Lowell Pratt & Co. Inc. | 15 East 48 Street, New York, N.Y. 10017 |
| Prentice-Hall, Inc. | Englewood Cliffs, N.J. 07632 |
| G. P. Putnam's Sons | 200 Madison Avenue, New York, N.Y. 10016 |

| | |
|---|---|
| Rand McNally & Company | P.O. Box 7600, Chicago, Ill. 60680 |
| Random House, Inc. | 457 Madison Avenue, New York, N.Y. 10022 |
| Reader's Digest Services, Inc. | Educational Division, Pleasantville, N.Y. 10570 |
| The Reilly & Lee Co. | 114 West Illinois Street, Chicago, Ill. 60610 |
| Reinhold Publishing Company | 430 Park Avenue, New York, N.Y. 10022 |
| John F. Rider Company, Inc. | 116 West 14 Street, New York, N.Y. 10011 |
| St. Martin's Press, Inc. | 175 Fifth Avenue, New York, N.Y. 10010 |
| Scholastic Book Services | 50 West 44 Street, New York, N.Y. 10036 |
| Science Research Associates, Inc. | 259 East Erie Street, Chicago, Ill. 60611 |
| William R. Scott, Inc. | 333 Avenue of the Americas, New York, N.Y. 10014 |
| Scott, Foresman & Company | 1900 East Lake Avenue, Glenview Ill. 60025 |
| Charles Scribner's Sons | 597 Fifth Avenue, New York, N.Y. 10017 |
| Silver Burdett Company | Morristown, N.J. 07960 |
| Simon & Schuster Inc. | 630 Fifth Avenue, New York, N.Y. 10020 |
| L. W. Singer Company (Division of Random House) | 501 Madison Avenue, New York, N.Y. 10022 |
| South-Western Publishing Co. | 512 North Avenue, New Rochelle, N.Y. 10801 |
| Sterling Publishing Company, Inc. | 419 Park Avenue South, New York, N.Y. 10016 |
| Teachers Publishing Corporation | 23 Leroy Avenue, Darien, Conn. 06820 |
| Frederick Ungar Publishing Co., Inc. | 250 Park Avenue South, New York, N.Y. 10003 |
| Vanguard Press, Inc. | 424 Madison Avenue, New York, N.Y. 10017 |
| D. Van Nostrand Co., Inc. | 120 Alexander Street, Princeton, N.J. 08540 |
| The Viking Press, Inc. | 625 Madison Avenue, New York, N.Y. 10022 |
| Time-Life Books (Division of Time, Inc.) | Time & Life Building, Rockefeller Center, New York, N.Y. 10020 |
| University of Washington Press | Seattle, Wash. 98105 |
| Harr Wagner Publishing Co. | 609 Mission Street, San Francisco, Calif. 94105 |
| Wadsworth Publishing Co., Inc. | Belmont, Calif. 94002 |
| Henry Z. Walck, Inc. | 19 Union Square West, New York, N.Y. 10003 |
| Watson-Guptill Publications, Inc. | 165 West 46 Street, New York, N.Y. 10036 |
| Franklin Watts (Division of Grolier) | 575 Lexington Avenue, New York, N.Y. 10022 |
| Webster Publishing (Division of McGraw-Hill Book Co.) | Manchester Road, Manchester, Mo. 63011 |
| Wesleyan University Press | 100 Riverview Center, Middletown, Conn. 06457 |
| Whitman Publishing Co. | 1220 Mound Avenue, Racine, Wis. 53404 |
| Whittlesey House (Division of McGraw-Hill Book Company) | 330 West 42 Street, New York, N.Y. 10036 |
| World Publishing Co. | 119 West 57 Street, New York, N.Y. 10019 |

*Film Distributors*

Academy Films, 1145 North Las Palmas Avenue, Hollywood, Calif.

Almanac Films, Inc., 29 East 10 Street, New York, N.Y.

Avis Films, Inc., P.O. Box 643, Burbank, Calif.

Bailey Films, Inc., 6509 De Longpre Avenue, Hollywood, Calif. 90028

Charles Cahill and Associates, 5746 Sunset Boulevard, Los Angeles, Calif. 90028

Cenco Films, Inc., 1700 Irving Park Road, Chicago, III.

Churchill Films, 662 North Robertson Boulevard, Los Angeles, Calif. 90059

Coronet Instructional Films, Coronet Building, Chicago, III. 60601

Dallas Jones Productions, Inc., 430 West Grand Place, Chicago, III.

Pat Dowling Pictures, 1056 South Robertson Boulevard, Los Angeles, Calif.

Educational Horizons, 3015 Dolores Street, Los Angeles, Calif.

Encyclopaedia Britannica Films, Inc., 425 North Michigan Avenue, Chicago, III. 60611

Film Associates of California, 11559 Santa Monica Boulevard, Los Angeles, Calif. 90025

Films, Inc. (see Encyclopaedia Britannica Films, Inc.)

Gateway Productions, Inc., 1859 Powell Street, San Francisco, Calif.

Jam Handy Organization, 2821 East Grand Avenue, Detroit, Mich. 48211

Peter Hollander, 80 Ellery Street, Cambridge, Mass.

Indiana University, Audio-Visual Center, Bloomington, Ind.

International Film Bureau, Inc., 332 South Michigan Avenue, Chicago, III. 60604

Journal Films, 909 Diversey Pkwy., Chicago, III. 60614

McGraw-Hill Book Co., Inc., 330 West 42 Street New York, N.Y. 10036

National Educational Television (see Indiana University)

Official Films, Inc., 776 Grand Avenue, Ridgefield, N.J.

Rampart Productions, 401 Taft Building, Los Angeles, Calif.

Tabletopper Productions, 111 East 6 Street, P.O. Box 706, Carson City, Nev.

United World Films, Inc., 1445 Park Avenue, New York, N.Y. 10029

Young America Films, Inc. (see McGraw-Hill Book Co.)

*Filmstrip Distributors*

Stanley Bowmar Co., Inc., 12 Cleveland Street, Valhalla, N.Y.

Canadian National Film Board, 1271 Avenue of the Americas, New York, N.Y.

Childrens Press, Inc., 1224 West Van Buren Street, Chicago, III. 60607

Creative Education, Inc., 340 North Milwaukee Avenue, Libertyville, III.

Curriculum Materials Corp., 119 South Roach Street, Jackson, Mich.

Encyclopaedia Britannica Films, Inc., 425 North Michigan Avenue, Chicago III. 60611

Eye Gate Productions, Inc., 146-01 Archer Avenue, Jamaica, N.Y. 91435

Filmstrip House, 432 Park Avenue South, New York, N.Y. 10016

International Visual Education Services, Inc., 300 South Racine Avenue, Chicago, III.

Jam Handy Organization, 2821 East Grand Avenue, Detroit, Mich. 48211

McGraw-Hill Book Co., Inc., 330 West 42 Street, New York, N.Y. 10036

Moody Institute of Science, 12000 East Washington Boulevard, Whittier, Calif. 90606

NET Film Service, Indiana University, Audio-Visual Center, Bloomington, Ind.

Charles Scribner's Sons, Educational Dept., 597 Fifth Avenue, New York, N.Y. 10017

Society for Visual Education, Inc., 1345 West Diversey Parkway, Chicago, Ill. 60614

Stillfilm, Inc., 35 South Raymond Avenue, Pasadena, Calif.

Young America Films, Inc. (see McGraw-Hill Book Co.)

Your Lesson Plan Filmstrips, 1319 Vine Street, Philadelphia, Pa.

## Equipment and Supply Distributors

Biological Supply Company, 1176 Mount Hope Rochester, N.Y.

California Biological Service, 1612 W. Glenoake Boulevard, Glendale, Calif.

Cambosco Scientific Co., Inc., 342 Western Avenue, Boston, Mass. 02135

Carolina Biological Supply Co., Elan College, N. Carolina

Central Scientific Co., 1700 Irving Park Road, Chicago, Ill.

Creative Play Things Inc., Edinburg Road, Cranbury, N.J. 08512

Denoyer-Geppert Company, 5235 Ravenswood Avenue, Chicago, Ill.

Fisher Scientific Company, 717 Forbes Avenue, Pittsburgh, Pa.

General Biological Supply House, 761 E. 69 Place, Chicago, Ill.

H. C. Hazel and Sons, Eustis, Fla. 32726

Hail Corporation, 210 S. Fourth Street, St. Louis, Mo.

Kuy-Sheerer Corporation, 2109 Borden Avenue, Long Island City, N.Y.

Macalaster Scientific Corp., Waltham Research and Development Park, 186 Third Avenue, Waltham, Mass. 02154

Macalaster Bicknell, Inc., 181 Henry Street, New Haven, Conn. 06511

Marine Biological Laboratory, Woods Hold, Mass.

National Biological Supply Co., Inc., 2325 South Michigan Avenue, Chicago, Ill. 60616

New York Biological Supply Co., 609 West 51 Street, New York, N.Y.

A. J. Nystrom and Company, 3333 Elston Avenue, Chicago, Ill.

Oregon Biological Supply Co., 1806 S.E. Holgate Boulevard, Portland, Ore.

E. H. Sargent and Company, 4601 W. Foster Avenue, Chicago, Ill.

Scientific Glass Apparatus Co., Bloomfield, N.J. 07003

Scientific Supplies Company, 173 Jackson Avenue, Seattle, Wash.

Southern Biological Supply Co., 517 Decatur, New Orleans, La.

Standard Scientific Supply Corp., 808 Broadway, New York, N.Y.

Stansi Scientific Co., 1231-41 North Honore Street, Chicago, Ill. 60022

University Apparatus Company, 229 McGee Avenue, Berkeley, Calif.

Ward's Natural Science Establishment, Inc., P.O. Box 24, Beechwood Station, Rochester, N.Y.

The Welch Scientific Company, 1515 Sedgwick Street, Chicago, Ill.

Western Laboratories, 826 Q. Street, Lincoln, Neb.

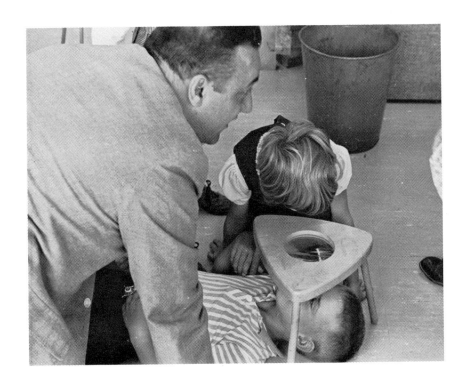

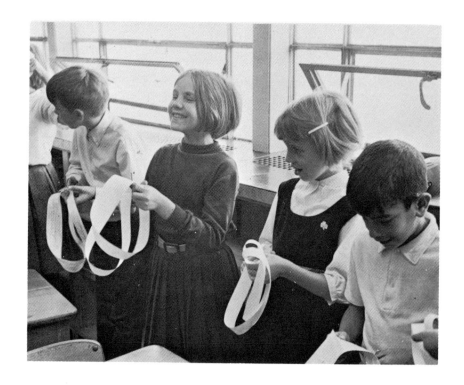